RESEARCHING TH
OF A COUNTRY H

C000292164

A guide to sources and their use

A house was useful first and beautiful second. From this derives the joy of visiting English houses. They are a conversation between utility and beauty down the ages. Through them we hear the echo of our collective selves – and remember who we are.

Simon Jenkins
(England's Thousand Best Houses, *Penguin/Allen Lane, 2003)*

RESEARCHING THE HISTORY OF A COUNTRY HOUSE

A guide to sources and their use

Richard Goodenough

 Phillimore

2010

Published by
PHILLIMORE & CO. LTD
Andover, Hampshire, England
www.phillimore.co.uk

ISBN: 978-1-86077-610-6

Printed and bound in Great Britain

ACKNOWLEDGEMENTS

Among the large number of people who have helped me to complete this book, I particularly wish to thank the following:

The staff of the Centre for Kentish Studies and
the Canterbury Cathedral Archives;
Bill Charlton, Arija Crux, John Hills, Roz
and, for his unflagging companionship, Sam.
I also acknowledge the support and design skills of Tim Ashenden,
of Mickleprint, in an earlier version of this book.

To my parents

Contents

List of Tables

List of Figures

An English home – gray twilight poured
On dewy pastures, dewy trees,
Softer than sleep – all things in order stored,
A haunt of ancient Peace.

Alfred, Lord Tennyson, 'The Palace of Art' (1832)

Introduction

The house historian has been compared to a detective following a trail, finding and evaluating evidence in order to confirm the age of a building, the names of residents who lived there, or the way of life they led in different historical periods. This approach has been successfully employed by Nick Barratt and popularised in the BBC television series *House Detectives*. The process of inquiry can be exciting with unexpected turns and consequences. It can also be frustrating as a lead turns cold and becomes a dead end, or sources cannot easily be found to provide an answer. There is no guarantee of success, but there will be surprises as you begin to throw light on the shadows of the past relating to the house and its occupants. Be warned, the process can be totally absorbing and extremely time-consuming – as well as fun!

The origins of this publication date from the late 1990s when I became interested in finding out more about an old house, Trimworth Manor, which we had recently bought. I am a geographer, not a historian, by training, but I found the early investigations into local history to be compelling, and began to see how I could use Trimworth as a case study in a voyage of discovery, which others could enjoy, by following a methodical and systematic process of research.

Trimworth is situated in a rural setting and has enjoyed a long and colourful history as a manor house. Initially, I felt I could apply the sources and techniques to any house in any location, but this was quickly found to be unrealistic. This publication is more relevant to the long-established country house, rather than a modern house in an urban setting. Some, but not all sources would be relevant to both situations, but it was felt desirable to maintain a focus rather than provide a broader approach to the house in general. Therefore, chapters will begin by discussing the nature of a specific source, followed by the application of that source to Trimworth. Availability of the various source materials will also be identified. This is not a comprehensive guide to all source materials, but a selection of those found to be most relevant and revealing to the study of Trimworth. Every house is unique, and it may well be that another researcher will uncover other sources appropriate to their own pathway of discovery. This is part of the research process. Have fun!

THE RESEARCH PROCESS, SOME POINTERS AND PITFALLS

It may be worth considering the following points at the planning stage.

- You should set realistic objectives, bearing in mind the time available and your budget. For example, your objective may simply be to find the date or dates of a building, using sources available near to home. Or you may want to trace the owners of your house from the present back to the date the house was built, using the census, wills and deeds, electoral lists, parish records, Chancery Rolls etc., some of which will require journeys to county or national archives. The list of sources in Table 1 is a useful summary of many sources used in this book and relates each source to a time period.

◆ Having set your objectives, try to stay focused. This is not easy, nor perhaps even essential, because other lines of inquiry may prove to be more attractive. However, try to avoid the 'kitchen sink' method, which may lead you beyond your time and cost constraints.

◆ Take time at the outset to locate research facilities and archive sources in your home area. They are likely to have a leaflet and/or website giving details of opening hours and documentary sources available.

◆ In general, it is wise to begin research at the local level, then broaden your search to county, regional and national archives, i.e. work from the 'known to the unknown'. The use of materials from your local library will give you a chance to get to know members of staff and feel more comfortable in a smaller local setting before possibly encountering a much larger and more intimidating national archive facility.

◆ Make a choice whether to start with the present and then work back in time, or begin at a point in time for which you have good information in the form of a map or document, and then work towards the present. Whichever approach you take, the results can be presented in a chronological form, or simply as a number of themes.

◆ Your first steps in research may involve talking to local people about your house and its history. They may be able to provide old photographs, names of former residents, etc. At the same time, investigate the history of the area and the social and economic changes that may have influenced the local environment and the people living within it.

◆ Be disciplined and methodical, particularly in keeping records. You must keep careful notes of archive reference numbers and published works in case you need to find them again. There are many personal preferences in the way records are kept, but there is no alternative to systematic and accurate recording of results.

◆ Be objective in your research, and do not confine your research to evidence that supports an already established hunch or idea. Do not dismiss conflicting evidence; you may have to consult a number of sources before you can corroborate a result with any certainty.

◆ Access to a computer, particularly for the internet, is very valuable and, with the growing availability of resources, almost essential. Archives are increasingly available online, and their use may obviate the need to travel so far or so frequently. Each chapter in this book will refer to internet sources, whether maintained

Table 1: Timeline of useful sources

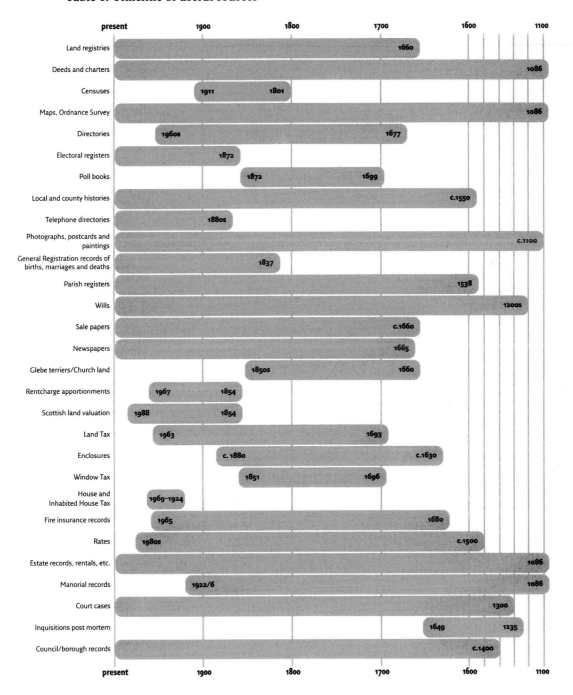

© Anthony Adolph, 2006

by professional organisations or archives offices. However, I hope you will still visit archives and consult sources at first hand. Just as the geographer needs to understand landscapes 'through the soles of his/her boots', so the local historian must consult primary sources, making their own conclusions rather than relying on the interpretation of someone else. Remember also that information found on a website does not come with a guarantee of accuracy. Be critical and double-check your sources for reliability.

Now it is time to get started!

CHAPTER I

Getting Started

ORAL HISTORIES

Talking to local people makes a refreshing change from hours spent searching through documents in the archives, and it is an activity which should come early in the research process because it may provide leads to follow up and avenues to pursue. A number of points may be helpful to bear in mind.

Do not miss the opportunity to talk to older locals. Shortly after moving into Trimworth we encountered the local shepherd, a source of endless information on changes in the rural scene, but I failed to record this information before he suddenly died and took a wealth of local knowledge with him. However, two local people with a good knowledge of Trimworth did provide some fascinating insights, and they are included here as examples of the kind of information which can be obtained through questioning local people. Joan Hartley was one of seven members of the Land Army living at Trimworth between 1942 and 1946. She was 17 and it was her first time away from home. Following two weeks training at Detling, she took up general farming duties of ploughing, sowing, looking after the pigs and running around the field waving arms to scare the birds away. Regular food parcels from home were joyously received and Saturday evening dances at Wye Village Hall eagerly awaited. The girls were paid monthly. One hot day Joan fell asleep turning the hay and had two hours' pay stopped. All meals were taken in the living room of Trimworth Manor. She remembers that 'two front rooms' were out of bounds except for courting! She rarely visited other rooms in the house but was aware of many empty rooms because farm personnel and family were away at war. Apart from the home sickness for two weeks, she remembers them as happy times with scenes of great activity on a busy farm raising crops and livestock.

The farm scene was delightfully retold by Gladys Pegden (Hann) who lived at nearby Little Olantigh and regularly visited her uncle, Walter Gibbons, the tenant at Trimworth. Walter had moved from Norfolk where he managed the Holkham Estate. The 1901 census shows Walter Gibbons as Head of House with a wife and nine children, ranging in age from one to 20, some of whom were Gladys Pegden's playmates. Walter quickly took an interest in local politics and in 1901, four years after he moved to Trimworth, he was elected Deputy Chairman of the Parish Council and Overseer of the Poor for many years. In 1912 the Gibbons family left Crundale and retired to a house in Upstreet, called 'Norfolk House' after his home county.

Gladys remembers the great fire at Olantigh in 1903, when her father helped to pull furniture out of the house and assisted the owner, Earle Drax, in saving a portrait of his wife. She remembers corn being taken from the farms to market in Faversham by horse-drawn carts, which were decorated with brasses, ribbons and bells. Families listened for the bells as the wagons returned down White Hill at the end of the day. Farm workers were paid about 18 to 20 shillings a week; most of them went to war in 1914. Four soldiers were billeted at Little Olantigh but Gladys saw little of them because she took over a great deal of the farm work, picking potatoes and looking after stock as well as walking to school at Wye. Father did little farm work; he was employed to protect local bridges during the day. There was no thought of holidays, her days began at 6 a.m. and they were long and tiring, punctuated with some high moments, such as salting down the pig for winter, the festivities of Cherry Sunday (Fig. 1), the summer show at Wye, shopping trips to Ashford, and the exploits of the Irish working on the railway. Saturday was payday for the Irish and all women were kept indoors!

These brief examples show how pictures of the local scene can help and avenues of enquiry identified. Remember, not all recollections may be accurate and there is a

1   Cherry Sunday at Little Olantigh Farm, 1909.
This is a celebration of the cherry harvest. Third from left on the back row is Henry Hann, the gamekeeper, who lived nearby at Longport. Seventh from left is 'Cherry Charlie'. Extreme right is William Hann, the farmer. In front are various grandchildren of William and Elizabeth Hann. (With acknowledgement to Mrs Gladys Pegden (Hann)).

2 Trimworth, 1950 and 2008.
Such photographic comparisons can illustrate change in both the landscape and economic activity of local areas.

need to check with official sources for hard facts. It is also worth remembering that locals may have their own private archives, such as photographic collections. Portraits and family groups may reveal information about interiors, while glimpses of buildings and gardens illustrate former economic activity and landscape change (Fig. 2).

Old postcards, sketches and paintings can also be useful sources, showing characteristics of your local area. Markets and bookshops frequently have specialist postcards and picture sales (see www.memoriespostcards.co.uk). A good illustration of what can be achieved by a diligent photograph search is Rex Lancefield's book *Pictures of the Past*

(1996), which is a fascinating collection of 160 pictures representing village life around Wye, including Crundale. Another publication by the same author, *Within Living Memory* (1990), is an impressive outcome of research involving oral histories which has provided a number of lines of enquiry on Trimworth. Equally impressive is *Tell us about when you were young*, compiled by Ann Pope and published by the Canterbury Environment Centre in 1997. It is a series of oral recollections of people from all social classes who worked in Canterbury and the surrounding countryside from 1900 to 1939. It is a perfect illustration of the value of local inhabitants as a starting point for research before moving on to other primary sources at the local records office.

LOCAL HISTORIES

Your local library will be a good source of local history, providing essential background information on your community as a starting point in your research. Although they may not mention your house, they will tell you about important events which have influenced your local community, such as population growth and decline, the role of major landowners in influencing land use change, or the impact of new modes of transportation, such as the rail network. This important preliminary exercise will develop your research skills in the local library and familiarise you with the background of the area. It is also worth consulting maps of different scales to become familiar with administrative boundaries, such as parish boundaries, the basic unit on which much information is expressed.

There has been a revolution in the availability of website information on local and community histories which should be explored. An excellent start would be: **www.visionofbritain.org.uk**, which enables you to enter a place-name or postcode for a whole range of data on the following themes:

Population: census data, often presented within the original tables.

Maps: the boundaries of parishes shown on 19th- and 20th-century maps.

Historical descriptions: extracts from Gazetteers and travellers' tales from the 12th to the 19th centuries.

Social class: information on socio-economic groups, from professionals to unskilled labourers.

Agricultural and land use: use of land for crops and animals.

Industry: how people in the past made their living, identifying farming communities, pit villages, mill towns, etc.

Housing: number of houses, measures of overcrowding such as persons per room, amenities.

The National Monuments Record also has a new website called **Pastscape** (www.pastscape.org), providing information about local history and archaeology on your doorstep, and covering a wide period of time from ancient history to Victorian times. This is a valuable tool for local history researchers.

Also, check **www.british-history.ac.uk**, which is a digital library offering access to a wide range of primary source material. It offers access to two 19th-century Ordnance Survey maps of the whole of Britain at a 1:10,560 scale and maps of major urban regions at 1:2,500 scale.

For those living in Kent, the website **www.hereshistory.kent.org.uk** contains a vast range of local history material for the towns and parishes of Kent, whether the subject of your research is house history or family history. The site provides a core of sources and links for both the casual and serious student of local history.

Using the Archives

Your first visit to an archives collection may be an intimidating experience, but you will soon become familiar with the procedures and gain confidence as you search for, and handle, the amazing amount of documentation available. Archives exist at a number of 'levels', and it is wise to begin at the local level such as **the town** or **city library**, or **local studies resource centre.** Take advantage of these facilities as soon as you can, and enquire about leaflets or special collections on local history and the way collections are indexed. At the next level is the **county record office**, or CRO, which will hold a greater range of documents and archival sources. Kent has three such centres, at Canterbury, Maidstone and Whitfield near Dover. The collections span 13 centuries and are a priceless source of first-hand information about people, places and events (Fig. 3). Most CROs will produce various leaflets on subjects such as family history, house history, poverty, crime, education, architecture, town planning, landownership, agriculture and industry. They will also offer excellent advice, provide a paid research service if required, and help educational users of all ages. **National Archives and Libraries** are the highest level of research facility, and should be consulted only when local and county sources have been fully explored. The National Archives are located at Kew, Surrey, and contain one of the largest archival collections in the world, spanning 1,000 years of British history. If you need help finding a document relating to the period after 1688 go to the **Research Enquiries Room**. Before this date, the **Map and Large Document Reading Room** is likely to be the most helpful. The **Microfilm Reading Room** will give access to information on births, marriages and deaths for family history research. First-time users of the National Archives should ask for a leaflet on 'New Reader Information' by telephoning 0208 876 3444. This will give all the basic information on contact numbers, site maps, facilities available, location and opening hours. Alternatively, consult the website www.nationalarchives.gov.uk.

Whichever facility you decide to use, the following points may be helpful to consider:

- Archives are busy places, and you may need to telephone ahead to reserve a seat, especially if you wish to use a microfilm reader.

- Most archives are only accessible if you have a reader's ticket. County archives are part of a network (County Archives Research Network), and your ticket will be valid at all facilities. Tickets can usually be issued when you arrive, but

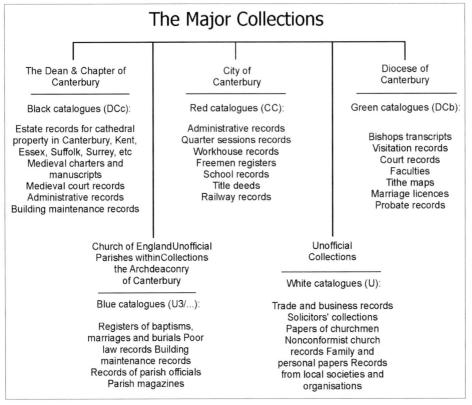

The Major Collections

The Dean & Chapter of Canterbury

Black catalogues (DCc):

Estate records for cathedral property in Canterbury, Kent, Essex, Suffolk, Surrey, etc
Medieval charters and manuscripts
Medieval court records
Administrative records
Building maintenance records

City of Canterbury

Red catalogues (CC):

Administrative records
Quarter sessions records
Workhouse records
Freemen registers
School records
Title deeds
Railway records

Diocese of Canterbury

Green catalogues (DCb):

Bishops transcripts
Visitation records
Court records
Faculties
Tithe maps
Marriage licences
Probate records

Church of England Parishes within the Archdeaconry of Canterbury

Blue catalogues (U3/...):

Registers of baptisms, marriages and burials Poor law records Building maintenance records
Records of parish officials
Parish magazines

Unofficial Collections

White catalogues (U):

Trade and business records
Solicitors' collections
Papers of churchmen
Nonconformist church records Family and personal papers Records from local societies and organisations

check whether you need passport photos and/or other forms of identification. The National Archives will require a reader's ticket, issued on arrival, with proof of identity.

- On your first visit, ask about the way materials are indexed. (There will probably be leaflets dealing with this.) The indexes are a key component of your search and may be in the form of index cards or bound volumes. Each item will have a reference number which you will have to provide to request materials. There are likely to be useful starting indexes on parishes, place-names, house names, manors and other materials. The more familiar you are with the archive index system the more fruitful will be your research.

- Before you visit, check that you have all the equipment you need, such as graphite pencils and plenty of paper. Erasers and pencil sharpeners may be forbidden on conservation grounds, as is food and drink, but laptops are usually permitted. Take notes with you on the topics you are researching, and a list of questions you may need to ask during your visit.

- Take care in handling documents. Avoid touching or leaning on the document, use reading aids, ensure documents are supported and do not lick fingers before turning pages. You may be required to use cotton gloves, especially when handling old or fragile documents and photographs, but staff will be available to assist and advise.

- Check on the policy of the archive regarding the use of cameras. They are likely to flexible about their use, especially for personal research. Your time in the archives is precious and it makes good sense to take photographs and obtain photocopies of maps and documents which can then be studied at leisure at home.

- Your excitement at discovering an interesting document may be tempered by finding it difficult to read because of poor handwriting or the use of letters in a different form, or the document is in Latin. Deciphering old writing is known as paleography (Fig. 4). Local and county record offices generally run short courses on paleography, and there are books which will help, for example, H. Marshall, *Palaeography for Family and Local Historians* (2004), published by Phillimore.

Another problem which may arise is unfamiliarity with measures and denominations. Money, for example, may be expressed as £6 3s. 6d., or in Roman numerals, vi, iii, vi. Land measurements may be in rods, poles, perches, roods, furlongs or other unfamiliar units. Again, books will help, such as C.R. Chapman, *How Heavy, How Much and How Long: Weights, Money and Other Measures Used By Our Ancestors* (1955), published by Lochin. Dates in old documents usually count from the date of the sovereign's accession, for example, 1 James 1st is the first year of James I's accession to the throne (i.e. 24 March 1603 to 23 March 1604). The start of the year has also changed; until 1752 the year began on 25 March rather than 1 January.

All these and other problems which you may encounter using archives will inevitably ease with growing use and familiarity with documents. It will also be reassuring to know that, in my experience, archive staff are unfailingly patient and polite, helpful and knowledgeable. Please respect their professionalism and reciprocate their courtesy.

4 Alphabet of post-medieval letter forms.
Alphabet of post-medieval letter forms, from A. Wright, Court Hand Restored *(1818), originally reproduced in H.E. Grieve,* Examples of English Handwriting *(Essex Record Office, 1954). Copies of this book are available from the E.R.O.*

The Internet

The potential of the Internet for undertaking research is widely recognised in terms of speed, accessibility and breadth of resources. Running a keyword search will reveal many useful sites of information, but you must be critical in your use of this information and be aware that some sites, often those set up by an enthusiastic individual, may not be accurate. It is wise to check information and facts with other sources to verify accuracy. There are many reliable official websites of professional organisations and institutions which will be referred to in later chapters. Increasingly, many archives are placing their catalogues online and can be consulted prior to a visit. The **National Access to Archives Project** (www.a2a.org.uk) contains catalogues describing archives held in over 400 local and county record offices, universities and specialist institutions. The system uses a keyword search; for example, 'Trimworth Manor' resulted in two 'hits', both being estate sales particulars for the years 1911 and 1920, held in the English Heritage National Monuments Record. The search facility is regularly updated, and so far has registered 131 million searches and 32 million downloads. The National Archives also provides online access to a wide range of digitised records such as wills, censuses, Domesday Book, etc. Searches are usually free; downloads and images are for a small fee. There are usually links to other related official websites.

Finally, the History Channel has recently set up a wonderful project called **Hidden House History** (www.hiddenhousehistory.co.uk), which allows you to search a series of 'best practice' and explore timelines of examples of case studies of house history in your local area. The site also gives you information about the tools you need to get started on researching house history (the people, the architecture, the local community). Experts such as Nick Barrett will take your researches further with help and advice. You will also learn how to unearth documents and identify architectural evidence to find out when your house was built.

Clearly the internet is a very valuable source of information, but it should not be your only source. There is no substitute for visiting archives and handling original documents. I will never forget the thrill of handling a 1607 conveyance for Trimworth from which hung the huge personal seal of James I, or holding an original parchment of an Anglo-Saxon Charter of 824 on which is written the name of 'Dreaman wyrthe' (Trimworth). The successful researcher will inevitably consult a range of source materials, primary and secondary, online and first-hand, in order to arrive at accurate and comprehensive conclusions.

CHAPTER 2

Historical descriptions and travels

Chapter 12 will refer to the county maps of Saxton (produced between 1574 and 1579), Speed (from the 1590s), and those more closely related to Kent, such as Andrews, Dury and Herbert (1769), and Hasted (1797). In addition to these map sources, many counties also have a collection of county histories or personal travels, likely to be housed in county archives or main libraries. They may not mention a specific property unless the house had an important history, but they are still good for providing an evocative background to the community and the environment in which your house is located. They can also be useful in providing maps and statistical summaries of populations, agriculture, industries, and other social and economic aspects of your community at different points in time, and may well identify source materials which you can follow up for more specific leads. This chapter selects a number of such histories and travels, with Kent as the chosen county, and referring, where possible, to Trimworth, located in the parish of Crundale.

COUNTY HISTORIES

'Among the different counties of England which have at times been illustrated by the labours of ingenious men, the County of Kent … has perhaps the greater share of their attention than any other kingdom.' This is the preface to *The History and Topographical Survey of the County of Kent*, written by Hasted and published in 1797. He also highlights the travels of Leland, librarian to King Henry VIII, and Camden, who published *Britannia* in 1586, subsequently published in five editions. Both are descriptions of the realm, and the county coverage is superficial and secondary. However, in 1570, William Lambarde, who had begun a topographical dictionary of the country, eventually published a volume on his own county of Kent. Hasted considers this to be a forerunner of other county histories, and it was also greatly admired by Camden. Camden's assistant, John Philpot, began making a study of Kent in 1619, but his efforts were overtaken by personal misfortune and the Civil War, and he died in poverty in 1645. His son, Thomas Philpot, continued the work, and in 1659 published *Villare Cantianum*, or *Kent Surveyed and Illustrated*. This is a survey of the tenants of several manors and landowners, together with historical discussions on sites of antiquity. A fascinating and unusual interpretation of the countryside is presented by Ogilby in 1675, with the publication of *Britannia*, which was a landmark in the mapping of England and Wales and now probably the most widely sought after

5   Ogilby Route Map, 1675, extract of 'London to Hithe', from *Britannia*.
The complete map begins in Cornhill, London, and traces the 69 miles and four furlongs in a continuous strip, at a scale of one inch to one mile.

collection of antique maps. Basically it is a national road atlas, composed of 73 major roads in continuous strip form at a scale of one inch to one mile. The maps record details of the countryside, such as local landmarks, houses, inns, bridges, fords and relief. There are comments on the state of cultivation and sketches of rural scenes. This is a wonderful impression of the face of the English countryside as seen by the 17th-century traveller and in a form that was comprehensible to the contemporary student. Of direct relevance to Kent is the route from London to Dover, pictured on six cartographic strips (Fig. 5).

Hasted: *The History and Topographical Survey of the County of Kent*

Hasted was born in London and educated at the King's School Rochester and Eton, before joining the legal profession at Lincoln's Inn. He returned to his parents home at Sutton At Hone and, after marrying, acquired the Knights Hospitaller's Manor House, where he wrote his *magnum opus*, the history of Kent. In 1770 he moved to Canterbury and lived there until 1789. During this time he sank deeper into debt despite selling some of his estates. He spent seven years in a debtors' prison, and after his release in 1802 he lived in poverty. He was given the mastership of an arms house in Corsham, Wiltshire, by a friend, and remained there as master until his death in 1812, aged 79.

Hasted's history of Kent was published in 1788 to 1799 in four volumes. A second edition, much revised, was published in 12 volumes between 1797 and 1801. There was a modern printing of his work in 1972. His survey is a major work comprising 7,000 pages; his manuscript notes ran to 100 volumes. The work covers every hundred and parish and was compiled and written entirely by Hasted himself from field observation and a huge range of archival sources. It is more than just a history, because it includes many contemporary maps as well as topographical descriptions of the state of the county. The period in which it was written was one of unprecedented change, with the population practically doubling between 1750 and 1801. Hasted captures this and many other changes and portrays the characteristics of regional diversity within the county in the late 18th century. He demonstrates the value of county history to the house researcher, and this will be illustrated now by reference to the parish of Crundale and the house of Trimworth.

The parish of Crundale merits 13 pages in Hasted, initially described as 'A small parish containing within it not more than 24 houses'. The landscape description is not encouraging, being 'exceedingly cold', 'exceedingly barren', with a 'wild and dreary appearance'. (His descriptions of many parishes refer to wildness and remoteness, one of the overriding characteristics of much of Kent.) A detailed description of archaeological finds is given, including those on Trimworth Down, referred to in Chapter 3. There is a fascinating reference to Trimworth Manor in which he notes:

> the old mansion has been moated around, and many fragments of the arms of Kempe are still remaining both in the windows and carve work of the wainscot and timbers of the house. It had formally a domestic chapel belonging to it, some of the walls of which are still standing.

(The existence of a moat is supported by a field name, Moat Field, near to the house on the tithe map of 1839, but the present contours of the site suggest that a moat encircling the house would be unlikely.) The importance of the manor in past times is recognised by the statement that it 'was formally of such eminent account, that the whole parish was called by that name … Crundale is frequently referred to as lying in Tremworth.' There are several pages giving details of the tenants of Trimworth, beginning with Bishop Odo of Bayeux, half-brother to William the Conqueror, and the powerful Earl of Kent, and ending with Sir Beversham Filmer in 1797. The manors of Cakes Yoke, Winchcomb and Vannes are similarly described in terms of inheritance, the source presumably being official records such as the Inquisition Post Mortem and the Chancery Rolls. Crundale church is given prominence in terms of the building, but equally important is material on the value and use of rectory lands and the tithes due from local landowners. The charities given to the church by prominent landlords and rectors are listed, varying from trees in the churchyard (Sir Thomas Kempe) to a parochial library (the Reverend Foster). John Finch of Limne contributed the sum of 40 shillings, payable out of his lands at Crundale and Godmersham 'to two of the eldest, poorest, and most industrious labouring men in the Parish of Crundale, and who never received relief of this or any other parish, that is 20 shillings to each of them yearly on Christmas Day forever'. Of great significance to Trimworth is the record that the church remained 'in the patronage of the Lords of Trimworth Manor, with which it continued to like manner as has been already mentioned, till it came into the possession of the late Sir John Filmer, Bart., who by Will in 1796 devised it with that manor to his brother Sir Beversham Filmer, Bart. the present proprietor of it'.

Such content will stimulate and excite the house researcher to delve deeper into sources and follow-up leads. There will inevitably be dead ends and occasionally confusion caused by inconsistent and inaccurate information. Hasted's work received pejorative comment from contemporaries, who described him as 'hasty', 'careless' and 'lacking critical ability', but his reputation grew to a point where his work became greatly admired, not for the (rather dull) nature of his prose, but for the enormous diligence in producing one of the finest county histories ever written. 'His laborious history of Kent took up more than forty years, during the whole of which he spared neither pain nor expense to bring it to majority.' These are the words of Hasted himself, which he instructed his executor to use for his obituary!

Victoria County Histories (VCH)

The VCH was founded in 1899 and dedicated to Queen Victoria, the aim being to produce an encyclopaedic history in sets of volumes covering each county. Publication continued slowly, and by 1914 six counties had been completed and over 80 volumes produced. Volumes are still being produced today under the co-ordination of the Institute of Historical Research, University of London, Senate House, Mallet Street, WC1E 7HU, Tel.: 0207 8628770. In February 2005, the

Heritage Lottery Fund awarded the VCH over £3 million pounds to further its work and promote public access to its research. This has been facilitated by the website, **www.englandspastforeveryone.org.uk**, where academic historians work with local volunteers to create a range of resources such as books, education packs for schools and volunteer programmes. The site also encourages interactive work on exploring maps, documents, and audio-visual aids. County contact details and on-going county projects are listed. For example, in Kent, the main project focuses on the lower Medway with 'now and then' photography of Halling, findings of a village survey in Eccles, a case study of the Burnham Cement Works, and the history of the Hook family of Snodland. The team leader is Dr Sandra Dunster, tel.: 020 8331 8962.

The three VCH volumes for Kent were published over a period from 1908 to 1932, and are arranged as follows:

- Volume 1 (1908) is a series of reports on pre-history, earth works, natural history, political and economic history. The state of agriculture, forestry, and other aspects of the economy provide a useful synopsis of the county at the turn of the 19th century.

- Volume 2 (1926) is an ecclesiastical history of the county with a description of religious houses including the College of Maidstone founded by Boniface, Archbishop of Canterbury. It was to this college that the manors of Tremworth and Vannes, together with the advowson of the church of Crundale, were granted by Richard II on the death of Henry Yevele in 1400.

- Volume 3 (1932) begins with an account of Romano-British Kent, including a description of all finds in the county, including Crundale. Then follows the Domesday survey of Kent and a political history. Of particular interest to the house historian is the section on social and economic history, containing information on parishes, such as parish population (1801-1921). Old deeds and manorial records are also covered, with chapter footnotes often including references to individual buildings and homes.

Other county histories for Kent

W.H. Ireland, *A New and Complete History of the County of Kent*, 1829-31

Described as a new and complete history of Kent and embellished with a series of views from original drawings, these volumes are most useful in the descriptions of individual parishes. For Crundale, the text describes the church and its patronage of Trimworth Manor under the Filmer family. Useful census information about the population of parishes is included. In 1821 there were 29 dwellings in the parish of Crundale and at the same period, when the last census of the population was undertaken by order of Parliament, the number of inhabitants was as follows: 'Males 123, Females 127, making a total of 250 soles.' Historical information is given for the manors in the parish collected from public records.

Samuel Bagshaw, *History, Gazetteer and Directory of the County of Kent,* **1847**

The work is published in two volumes, again providing parish information on population, landownership (farmers are named), poor of the parish, charities, occupation and trade of inhabitants, market days and stock markets.

Samuel Lewis, *A Topographic Dictionary of England*, **1848**

This publication gives a historical and contemporary description of counties, cities, parishes, towns, villages and hamlets across the whole of mid-19th-century England. The volumes complement earlier histories of the Lyson brothers, *Magna Britannia*, and the later, more detailed, Victoria County Histories. Lewis's work is now digitised and is available online at **www.british-history.ac.uk** together with other core primary and secondary sources for medieval and modern history. It is free of charge.

TRAVELLERS' TALES

A valuable source of economic and social history is found in the journals of travellers such as Daniel Defoe (1724-6) and Celia Fiennes (1680-1700), both of whom recorded detailed observations of Kent. A little later we encounter William Cobbett, born in 1763, son of a yeoman farmer who travelled on horseback through England recording his observations just before the railways spread their network and changed the face of England.

William Cobbett, *Rural Rides*

Cobbett was the son of a farmer who fled to the United States after 'blowing the whistle' on military corruption in the army. He returned in 1800 and became a champion of traditional rural society at the time of its imminent transformation by the Industrial Revolution. He was a grass-roots radical, a supporter of labourers' rights, and his observations reveal his love of the countryside rather than towns. The town of Sandwich is described 'as villainous a hole that one would wish to see, surrounded by some of the great lands in the world'. Deal has even less to commend it, being 'a villainous place of filthy looking people, everything seems upon the perish'. These observations are recorded in a ride he took on September 1823 from Dover to the Isle of Thanet, then on to Canterbury, Faversham, Maidstone and Tonbridge, passing through the Weald of Kent to London ('the Wen'). He describes the sheep farming of Romney Marsh and the importance of hops around Canterbury and Maidstone, giving details of yields and returns. Highest praise is recorded for fruit. 'The fruit in Kent is more select than Herefordshire where it is raised for cider, while in Kent it is raised for sale in its fruit state … the orchards are beautiful indeed, kept in the neatest order, and indeed all belonging to them excels anything of the kind to be seen in Normandy, as to apples I never saw any so good in France as those in Kent.' Descriptions of Cobbett's *Rural Rides* can be found at **www.visionofbritain.org.uk**, under the banner heading of 'Travellers' Tales'. Place-names are highlighted in each ride, and there are links to other sources of information on that particular place.

Charles Igglesden, *A Saunter through Kent with Pen and Pencil* (1939)

Occasionally, the process of research will unexpectedly reveal a treasure. Such is the case with this delightful set of volumes, written with a sympathetic and perceptive eye, and illustrated with superb pen and ink drawings. Igglesden's motive for this work is conveyed in the preface of the first volume. 'My idea in writing this saunter through Kent is to preserve a picture of our countryside as it appeared at the beginning of this century. As years roll by, changes are inevitable with the appearance of villages and towns, of our lanes, and other rural scenery and customs.' Just as Cobbett wrote on the eve of the Industrial Revolution, Igglesden's publication in 1939 was followed by another phase of conflict and turmoil on a scale which was impossible to envisage, making this 'snapshot' of Kent even more endearing and significant. The preface to Volume 32, which includes the parish of Crundale and makes specific reference to Trimworth, is a wonderful description of the Downs extending between Hastingleigh and Stone Street.

6 Trimworth in 1939, from a sketch in Igglesden's *Saunters Through Kent*.
A delightful set of volumes providing a synoptic view of Kent on the eve of the Second World War.

TRIMWORTH

It is one of the most thinly populated parts of Kent, and therein lies its charm. The pastures and wooded slopes are alluring in their peacefulness and rural simplicity, dotted with a solitary homestead here and there, wide links that join up with villages, or rather hamlets, still sleeping and undisturbed by the turmoil of the busy world. Each village possesses its parish church and it's non-conformist chapel, the pride of the people of the countryside still imbued with the religious fervour that their ancestors enjoyed. Here too, we find the type of farmer that not only loves his native soil, but takes a pride in historic and picturesque charm of his old world homestead. Here, on the top of the Downs or down in the valleys, you will find peace.

The volumes are of great value to the house historian, describing many houses in each parish, occasionally referring to Hasted, but also to comments of owners at the time. Referring to the old domestic chapel at Trimworth,

Mr James Hodgson, who at present lives there, has found some flint foundations in an adjoining field. There was at one time some wainscotting carved with the arms of Kempe, and the explanation of its disappearance is that much of the panelling was sold to an American, who about fifty years ago, bought up other carving in the Tudor buildings in the neighbourhood.

A little bit of Olde England in the New World, and hopefully being valued in its new setting as much as it would have been here! Igglesden's treasured writings are liberally interspersed with excellent sketches, such as the one of Trimworth, included here, drawn with some artistic licence (Fig. 6).

This chapter has reviewed county histories and their content as an illustration of how a secondary source can provide useful detail on the community and environment in which your house is located. It is a library-based, preliminary research activity. The next chapter is concerned with the landscape itself, as a source of evidence for earlier occupation and land use, and an influence on the location of your house. Trimworth will be used as a case study.

CHAPTER 3

The Landscape as a Document

Below the bricks and mortar of our built environment lies another landscape, influenced by both geology and perhaps previous inhabitants who left their mark as a sequence of occupation from prehistory to the present. The face of the open countryside also bears the imprint of ancestors who have farmed, mined and built communities, leaving their imprint in the form of old field boundaries, building lines, worked-out pits and archaeological sites. W.G. Hoskins' wonderful book, *The Making of the English Landscape*, narrates the historical evolution of the countryside, describing and explaining the origins of hedge banks, woodlands, ruined churches, field patterns, field boundaries, hamlets and towns. It is a classic, bringing together the disciplines of history and geography to understand the chronological development of the English landscape.

At an early stage in research on house history, it is a valuable exercise to consider the location of your house in relation to its site and situation, local geology, drainage patterns, landforms, soils and the evidence in the locality of former societies. This evidence may be revealed through descriptions of previous archaeological investigations, geophysical surveys or aerial photographs and maps. Trimworth Manor and its surrounding environment will be used as a case study in order to identify the sources available, and exemplify their use in setting the scene before a more detailed focus on the structure of the house itself in Chapter 4.

TRIMWORTH AND ITS SURROUNDING ENVIRONMENT

Trimworth lies within the Stour valley where the river cuts through the chalk of the North Downs, a location which has had great historical and geographical significance. The house is located on a river terrace 30m above sea level and 200m from the river. Across the river to the west the land rises up to the Godmersham Downs reaching a height of 146m in Kings Wood. To the east a more gradual slope rises up to Trimworth Downs. Both downland landscapes have a rich archaeological heritage, and provide shelter for the fertile river meadows lying below (Figs 7 and 8). From both chalk downs there are extensive views up and down the river to which Hasted referred with enthusiasm in his 18th-century history of the county.

> From the high road which runs along the lower side of the western hills there is a most pleasing view over the valley beneath, in which various beautiful objects of both art and nature combine to make it the most delightful prospect that can be imagined.   (Hasted, 1798)

7 Trimworth's site and situation from Trimworth Downs.
A view looking west across the Stour Valley, to Kings Wood on the Godmersham Downs. Trimworth is located middle distance on the right. Note the importance of the valley as a road, rail and river routeway through the North Downs.

The landscape is strongly influenced by the geological structure of the area. The underlying geology is chalk, composed of marine sedimentary formations of the Cretaceous period into which the River Stour has cut to breach the North Downs escarpment. On the surface of the solid geology there are superficial deposits such as river terrace gravels, head brickearth and 'clay-with-flints' which have affected the landforms and soils of the area around Trimworth. The slopes of the Downs above Trimworth are further characterised by dry valleys or coombes, formed during an extremely cold period when meltwater on frozen chalk eroded steep-sided valleys.

8 Trimworth, site and situation from Godmersham Downs.
Looking east towards Trimworth Downs, with a glimpse of the Stour, and Trimworth middle distance in centre.

9   Dry Valley, Trimworth Downs.
The gentle slopes a nd thin soils marking one of the many dry valleys, excavated when the normally permeable chalk was frozen.

A prominent example is the dry valley running west from Trimworth Down, passing the northern edges of Black Edge Wood, Oxen Lees Wood and Tye Wood before passing close to Trimworth Manor to join the Stour Valley (Fig. 9).

It is the superficial deposits that have influenced the variety of soil types in the area. In places, rainwater dissolving the calcium carbonate has left a residue of clay, stained brown by the acid and containing irregular flints from the upper chalk. This 'clay-with-flints' has presented a challenge to the Trimworth gardeners. More welcome is the brickearth deposit which forms a thin but fertile topsoil as well as an ideal medium for bricks. The location of Trimworth next to the river provides fertile, stoneless silts of river alluvium, above which gravelly river terraces form benches overlooking the valley floor, avoiding the risk of flooding (Fig. 10). The only common factor in this diversity of soils is the fact that most are calcareous, but otherwise they present a wide variety of soil type, structure and drainage over short distances, making the map of soils a misleading generalisation. For the gardener they offer the prospect of gentle cultivation with a border fork or an assault with a pick-axe to remove flint nodules set in heavy clay!

Map sources and availability

- **Ordnance Survey.** Check the website www.ordnance.co.uk for details of all products, services and prices.

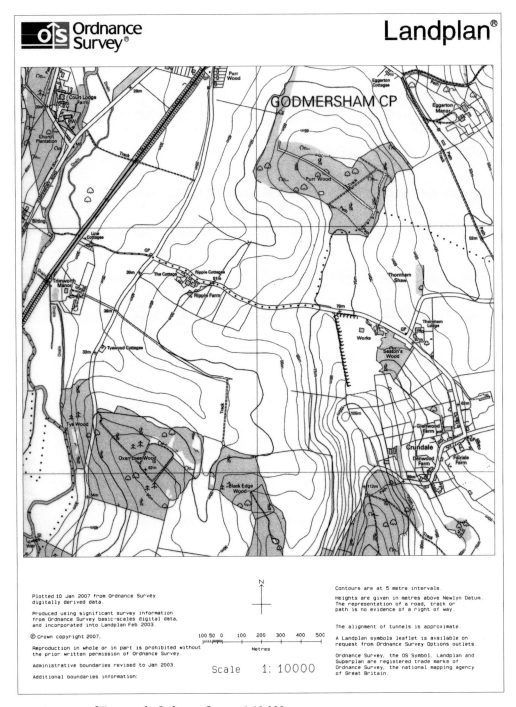

10   Location of Trimworth, Ordnance Survey, 1:10,000.
Trimworth is located on the western margin, 219m from the Stour and on a terrace between the 30m and 35m contours. (© Crown Copyright 2007, Licence 100047754)

- ◆ **British Geological Survey**. For site investigations, the Survey can provide reports containing map extracts at a scale of 1:50,000, with information on land-slips, solid and superficial geology displayed separately as 10x10cm extracts. See www.bgs.ac.uk for cost and availability.

- ◆ **Environment Agency.** The website www.environmentagency.gov.uk/maps will allow you to check 'what's in your backyard'. Especially useful is the availability of flood maps at a scale of 1:20,000. Check your neighbourhood, at no cost, by putting in a place-name or postcode.

LANDSCAPE HISTORY AND ARCHAEOLOGY

The topography of the area has strongly influenced the movement of people and the location of settlements, particularly the downland landscapes and the river valley. The evidence for this lies in the rich archaeological heritage dating back to prehistoric environments 10,000 years ago. A historic landscape survey of Godmersham Park and environs has been an important source of information on the landscape history of the area (Nicola Bannister, *Godmersham Park, Historic Landscape Survey*, 1995, funded by English Heritage), together with information from the National Monuments Records.

Prehistoric environments
Paleolithic and Mesolithic societies

The Paleolithic hunter worked in a very different environment to the one we know today. The climate was considerably cooler, characterised by a series of Ice Ages interspersed with more temperate periods. The vegetation, much more extensive than now, would have been dominated by pine and other soft woods. There is no recorded evidence of Paleolithic activity around Trimworth, although flint finds have been made in the Chilham area. More significant collections of flints from the Mesolithic period (10,000-6,000 B.P.) have been found beneath a Bronze-Age barrow at Olantigh and also at Buckwell Farm nearby. These people were hunters and gatherers, using flint implements to prepare meat and skins and to fashion weapons. Their imprint on the land was minimal because there were few permanent settlements. They followed seasonal migrations, obtaining food sources from a variety of habitats: streams, meadows, forests, woodland clearings and marshes. During this period, sea levels were rising because of glacial melt water, leading to increased isolation of human groups in Britain, the land bridge with Europe being breached about 8,300 B.P. to give Britain full insularity.

Neolithic societies (5,000-2,500 B.P.)

The slow transformation from a society that followed its food source to a more sedentary one concentrating on food production occurred during the Neolithic period, although it is likely that farming and hunter/gathering activities co-existed. The change brought with it a significant landscape transformation as woodland clearance quickened to provide cultivation, and more open chalk lands were cleared for the domestication of sheep, cattle and goats. Proximity to the continent meant that these new ideas were introduced early in Kent. The chalk downlands provided an obvious corridor for travel, being dry with good visibility and easy access to the spring-fed streams that emerge from the junction of chalk and clay. Neolithic people would thus have walked on this Trackway (more popularly called the Pilgrims Way) between the Wiltshire Downs and the continuation of the chalk outcrop into France (La Leulene). The Downs, gradually cleared for cultivation, were a mosaic of woodland, pasture and arable. Neolithic material is common in the area around Trimworth, reflecting these agricultural activities of the period.

No settlement sites have been found for these Neolithic farmers although their presence is suggested by a long barrow, Julieberrie's Grave, near Chilham, 44m long and 2.5m high and containing flint flakes, bones of oxen and sheep, and a flint axe of apparent Scandinavian affinity. More frequent finds of flint axeheads suggest their effectiveness as implements for forest clearance, and their widespread occurrence in the area (Chilham, Eggringe Wood, Godmersham, Devils Kneading Trough) is evidence of the extent of clearance and cultivation during this period.

Bronze-Age societies, 1,500-600 B.C.

The chemical composition of copper finds from this period indicates migration into the South East of England from the continental mainland. A bronze chisel found on the Wye Downs has been regarded as the earliest recognised metal import in Kent, probably originating from Germany. This wave of immigration brought the next phase of woodland clearance and the development of farming communities, some of whom produced surpluses for trade, obtaining status objects such as bronze ornaments and weaponry. Land, power and prestige had become key components of the Bronze-Age society, especially in the later Bronze Age. The Stour Valley provided a good trading route with the coast and its fertile soils encouraged settlement. Although there is no recorded evidence of Bronze-Age field systems or enclosures in this part of the Stour Valley, this does not mean that they did not occupy the area. There is plenty of evidence of burial sites on top of the Downs and on the valley sides. These sacred areas were used for multiple burials and cremations, sometimes in groups or in isolated locations on high ground where they have formed prominent landscape features. A common form is a bow shape encircled by a ditch, such as that to the west of Godmersham in Kings Wood. However, not all barrows were on high ground. To the southwest of Olantigh on the floor of the Stour is the site of a cremation barrow containing sherds of beaker-ware similar to those found in the Rhine area.

The closest Bronze-Age finds to Trimworth are located at Salterfen on the Canterbury Road (TR0598500), immediately below an old routeway which is reported to be of Roman age but is probably much older. Excavation was by the Ashford Archaeological Society in 1966-8. The pottery finds from this excavation are in the Maidstone Museum (see NMR Activity Report 638882, also *Archeologia Cantiana* 81/1967/L111 and 83/1969/253).

In September 2003 a metal detectorist, working on farmland a few hundred metres from Trimworth, unearthed significant finds which were reported to the Finds Liaison Officer, who came to the site. He uncovered a Bronze-Age hoard in a shallow pit just below the ploughsoil, consisting of 185 pieces of metalwork in the form of a cast copper cake with other artefacts above. Artefacts included rings, razors, axeheads, spearheads and fragments of swords and daggers typical of other

11 Bronze-Age hoard, 2003, Crundale.
This image of a socketed and tanged knife was one of 185 objects found in a shallow hollow. (With acknowledgement to Jim Bishop, the finder.)

Bronze-Age hoards found in the South East and traditionally described as 'Founder's Hoards' (Fig. 11). The Finds Liaison Officer suggests they could represent collections of scrap metal although other interpretations by experts have challenged this. An alternative view is that they have been deliberately broken in order to put them beyond use. In one instance objects have been driven into sockets of axeheads and spearheads. Whatever the situation, the find is extremely significant because of its size and the unusually varied items found, including copper alloy rings. Investigation of the site is ongoing and the exact location has not yet been disclosed.

Iron-Age societies (700 B.C. - A.D. 43)

A growing population and their use of iron implements, pottery and coinage were characteristic of Iron-Age communities who maintained close links with the continent via trading routes such as the Trackway, linking hill-forts and settlements with iron working of the Weald. The Stour would have been an important means of access inland as well as a source of fertile valley soils and adjacent chalk downland. Much of the population worked the land. Forest clearance continued, using better implements and requiring careful management of woodland as a fuel resource for the industry. On the chalkland soils, both animal husbandry and crop production would have been practised.

Early Iron-Age occupation was particularly dense in East Kent, especially the Isle of Thanet. Evidence of middle Iron-Age settlements is rare, confined largely to hill-forts such as Bigberry, Kent's most easterly hill-fort. Later Iron-Age settlement expanded into central and western Kent and during this period the production of

12 Iron-Age site on Trimworth Down.
Looking north towards Chilham from the crest of the Downs at 100m. Disturbed ground in the foreground is the result of previous diggings from which pot fragments and earth works have been found. Crundale chalk quarry in middle distance reveals shallow depth of soil.

grains, pottery and metal products allowed an export trade to develop, with a return flow of goods bringing new ideas and immigration. The area around Trimworth presents good evidence of Iron-Age occupation. An early Iron-Age settlement has been recorded just below the crest of Trimworth Downs at about 100m (Fig. 12). The find comprised pot fragments associated with possible earthworks, although there is little recorded detail of this. More significant is the extensive field system on the Godmersham Downs (Fig. 13), documented in Barringon's landscape history of Godmersham Park.

These Iron-Age fields represent an advance on the smaller, irregular corn plots of the Bronze-Age farmers. They are more or less rectangular blocks rarely more than 60m long and 30m wide. These ancient fields have survived because they are laid out

13 Iron-Age field systems, Godmersham Park.
The aerial photograph reveals glimpses of rectangular plots of an old field system which has survived despite centuries of more recent ploughing. The photograph was taken in 1979 and the location is TR057508.

on smooth short turf on the dry chalk soils and also because they were abandoned at a later date in favour of heavier, more productive soils in the valleys below.

Five curving lynchets varying in height from 2 to 3.5m and following the contours around the slope of Godmersham Down are also clearly visible. The lynchets extending along the east-facing slope of Godmersham Downs overlooking Trimworth are less well defined, but are clearly visible in low sunlight (Fig. 14). These lynchets abound in the chalk downlands of South East England as cultural formations on the natural slope. They represent the boundary between the ploughed fields and have been formed as a result of ploughing on a slope. The movement of soil downslope forms the boundary edge (positive lynchet) while below, ploughing, soil movement, trampling and rainwash undercut the slope (negative lynchet). The boundary remains undisturbed compared to adjacent ploughed soils and often contains archaeological evidence, especially when it has been grassed over for many years.

It is interesting to speculate on the scene between Godmersham Down and Trimworth Down during this period. Godmersham was probably well established as a small community situated in the sheltered valley and farming the fertile soils of the valley floor and terraces. The river acted as a vital waterway allowing trading of goods both upstream and downstream. A heavy iron plough would have been used to cultivate the heavier soils to produce corn in enough quantity to trade and export. Overlooking the valley was the downland through which ran important route ways, winding between small, cultivated fields, woodland clearances and forests. The native population were well organised into tribal groups and readily assimilated new

14 Lynchets, Godmersham Down.
Fields above Godmersham church show the effect of ploughing on steep slopes, producing a series of terraces.

ideas. So organised was the social and economic structure that much of it survived and was incorporated with Roman society.

Roman occupation (A.D. 43-410)

The period of Roman rule lasted nearly 400 years, during which time the map of Kent was transformed by the appearance of towns, transportation routes, industrial activity and major fortifications. This short review will concentrate on the rural landscape with particular reference to evidence of occupation in the area around Godmersham and Trimworth.

When Caesar reported on his journeys into Kent in 55 to 54 B.C., he noted that it was 'thickly studded with farmsteads'. Certainly, most of the best farmland was already under cultivation, but Roman occupation brought a new feature, the villa, varying in size from huge houses to modest farmhouses. In some cases the villas occupied the sites of earlier Iron-Age farmsteads. Their distribution in East Kent is sparse, with the exception of the Isle of Thanet. The vast majority of the population continued to live in native farmsteads which were very similar to those of the late Iron Age. The rural landscape was dominated, therefore, by isolated farmsteads consisting of a few wattle-and-daub huts roofed with thatch.

The cultivation of soils with the heavier plough opened up new lands that hitherto had been too intractable, and it is likely that this led to the increase in population. However, the population of Britain on the eve of the Roman conquest was probably less than 500,000. The first 2,000 years of farming from Neolithic times had still hardly left a mark on the landscape. Clearances, fields and settlements were locally important, but considered as a whole they had not made a huge impression on the natural landscape.

The River Stour continued to be a natural corridor for soldiers and settlers. It is likely that Caesar, having attacked the hill-fort at Bigbury, drove out the Britons and followed them along the Stour Valley or along the prehistoric trackway on the North Downs to the river crossing at Wye. There is strong evidence for Roman activity in the area around Trimworth. Most significant is the third-century Roman cremation or urn find with later Saxon burials located half a kilometre south of Trimworth Manor. The site is on a terrace overlooking the Stour on the edge of the land which is currently wooded (Oxen Leas Wood and Tye Wood, Fig. 15). At this site in 1703 a skull was found by a walker and, later, a human skeleton together with an urn of Roman origin. Nearby was a child's skeleton with a little red pot. The site was excavated by the local rector and in 1713 a grave dug into the chalk was found containing three urns. There were later excavations in 1757 and 1759 which are well documented (Audrey Meaney, *A Gazetteer of Early Anglo-Saxon Burial Sites* (1964), p.116).

These burials are probably associated with a Roman settlement site which was to be excavated by the Canterbury Archaeological Trust on Trimworth Downs following soil stripping at Crundale Lime Works. The excavation revealed cremation

15   River terrace, Tye Wood, Trimworth.
This terrace lies at about 30m above the flood plain of the River Stour, affording a dry site for settlement (Roman), and easy access to the river and its fertile valley.

burials, pottery scatters, linear ditches, post holes and pottery dating from the first to the fourth centuries. Further finds, attributed to the Saxon period, were found at the same site in 1858, illustrating the continuity of occupation over a long period. Among the finds was a bronze buckle plated with silver and gold and inlaid with garnets. The central spine of the buckle is a gold fish whose body is decorated with fine gold wire. The fish was an early Christian symbol and its use here may be a deliberate reference to Christianity. In this respect, the dating of the buckle to the early seventh century is significant because in 597 a Christian mission led by Saint Augustine landed in Kent to convert pagan Anglo-Saxons. The Crundale buckle may therefore be an indication of conversion to Christianity and the indirect social and economic changes which accompanied it. The buckle was found in a man's grave together with a garnet-inlaid copper alloy buckle and an iron sword with a decorated pommel, all purchased by the British Museum (on display in Room 41).

In describing these finds, this narrative has leapt from Romans to Anglo-Saxons, but the transition was, in fact, a gradual one. As central control from Rome weakened, the villa system began to decay and the military presence dissipated. Migration of Anglo-Saxons from Germany and Scandinavia to eastern England grew, and throughout the fifth and sixth centuries they gained domination over the indigenous population. Much of the cleared and farmed landscape had reverted to its natural state during the long transfer of power, but was to be transformed again by the open-field system of the Anglo-Saxon period. Anglo-Saxon settlements were established over a period between A.D. 450 and 1066, during which time England became a land of villages. We will return to this period with reference to an Anglo-Saxon boundary record featuring Trimworth Manor in the next chapter.

Sources for archaeology

The use of the National Monuments Record (England Heritage)

The National Monuments Record is England's national archive of heritage information, containing 12 million items covering archaeological sites, records for buildings (including the Listed Buildings Information Service), data on scheduled monuments and an extensive reference library. Use of the National Monuments Record is free at the search rooms at Swindon or London. Of particular value to the researcher is the free search service of archaeological sites which the National Monuments Record will undertake on your behalf. It is necessary to complete a search request form for the site or area under study. All enquires about the archaeological database should identify a single site or area, using a grid reference and indicating the radius of interest. There is no restriction on the size of the search area, but if the area is less than 25 square kilometers, an Index Report is provided free of charge. This will give all the recorded entries on a database, listing the description of the entry (e.g. a 17th-century house or an Iron-Age field system), location, period (e.g. post-medieval, Bronze-Age) and dates. The request made for Trimworth Manor produced an Index Report listing 29 monument entries and six entries in the Activities Index, (the latter costing 34p plus VAT per entry.)

Contacting the National Monuments Record

The Centre in Swindon is a short walk from Swindon railway station and ten minutes drive from Junction 16 of the M4. The address is:

NMR Public Services,
National Monuments Centre,
Great Western Village, Kemble Drive,
Swindon, SN2 2GZ
Tel.: 01793 414600
Email: nmrinfo@english-heritage.org.uk

The Public Search Room is open from 9.30 to 1700 on Tuesday to Friday.

The NMR in London is in Blandford Street near Baker Street underground station. The address is:

NMR Public Service,
55 Blandford Street, London, W1H 3AF
Tel.: 0171 208 8200; Fax: 0171 224 5333
Email: londonnmr@english-heritage.org.uk

The Public Search Room in London is open from 10.00 to 17.00 Tuesday to Friday.

Surveying Techniques in Landscape History

Geophysical surveying at Trimworth

In the summer of 2004, plans were being drawn up for the construction of a sunken garden at Trimworth, measuring 10 metres by five metres and a depth of one metre. This required a considerable amount of earth moving and alteration of the garden to the north of the house. It had always been conjectured that the domestic chapel, first mentioned in the Domesday Monachorum, was located on this side of the house. A map of 1680 (Fig. 54) shows an isolated building in this area, and Hasted also refers to the ruins of a chapel in an adjoining field, but it has been difficult to pinpoint the exact location from documentary or cartographic sources.

Before undertaking the earth works, a geophysical survey of the north side of the house was carried out, to ensure the construction of the sunken garden would not disturb any structural remains such as foundations, floors, or demolition rubble, etc. that might exist below ground. The technique and purpose of geophysical surveys, and reports on the findings at Trimworth undertaken on 10 October 2004, will now be discussed.

The technique

(For detailed reference to this technique, see K. Green, *Archaeology: an introduction* (2002), Ch. 2, London: Routledge). Very few archaeological sites reveal themselves fully in aerial photographs or in landforms, so it is often necessary to use geophysical prospecting techniques to explore invisible features of a buried site. The main purpose is to distinguish any anomaly, possibly of human origin, occurring in the natural sub-soil, using **resistivity survey** or **magnetometers**. The former measures the resistance of the sub-soil to the passage of an electric current, the latter detects variations in the sub-soil's magnetic characterstics. The method used at Trimworth was resistivity surveying, carried out by Neil and Fiona Griffin of the University College London Field Archaeology Unit. A baseline was established from which a 20-metre grid was laid out. Four probes were pushed into the ground at measured intervals and readings taken to show variations in resistance to the electric flow. A current will pass easily through damp soil, but drier, compact material such as a buried wall or rubble creates higher resistance. The method is quite cumbersome and is best suited to the detection of linear features such as walls or ditches. Furthermore anomalous readings (noise spikes) can occur with this technique, especially in areas with dense root growth or geological variation.

Results and interpretation

Fig. 16 shows the survey location, and should be used with Fig. 17, the interpretation of the field survey. High resistance readings were obtained over a linear bank within grids 1 and 3, whereas at the bottom of the slope to the west lower readings were recorded. This supports the view that the earthwork is made up of more freely draining material in comparison to the bottom of the slope. The northern corner of

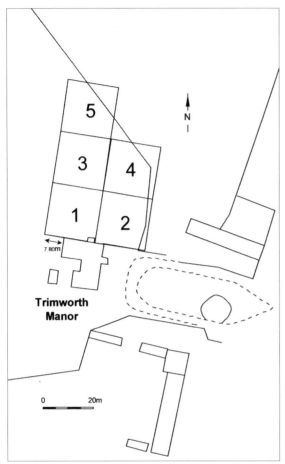

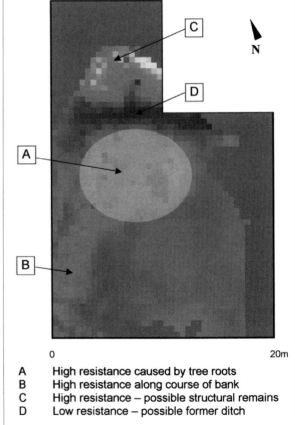

16   Geophysical survey, Trimworth, 2004.
Location of survey plots.

A	High resistance caused by tree roots
B	High resistance along course of bank
C	High resistance – possible structural remains
D	Low resistance – possible former ditch

17   Analysis of geophysical survey of Trimworth.
The area marked 'C' has readings which suggest the structural remains of a building, possibly the former chapel mentioned in Domesday and subsequent documents.

the garden within grid 5 gave the highest resistance readings in the surveyed area. This was immediately flanked to the south by what appears to be a roughly east-to-west line of low resistance, the lowest obtained on the site. The higher resistance readings may indicate building remains, and they continue beyond the property boundary into an adjoining field. They appear to form two distinct linear shapes at approximate right angles and may represent walls, or discrete areas of rubble. The low-resistance area may indicate the presence of a silted up former ditch and could represent a former boundary.

The conclusion to this survey is as follows:

- Three features of interest were identified, two possibly relating to structural remains, and one possibly representing a former ditch.

- Further survey is needed to extend the search into the adjoining field.

- Exploratory trenching could be the next step in determining the nature of features of interest.

- No site of interest was identified in the location of the planned sunken garden, which has now been completed.

THE USE OF AERIAL PHOTOGRAPHY

The technique

Aerial photography has made a huge contribution to archaeology, bringing to light buried sites that would otherwise be difficult to detect through field work or field walking. Reconnaissance photography for strategic purposes was carried out during the First World War, with the emphasis on map-making rather than archaeological research. The comprehensive coverage by the RAF after the Second World War has provided a marvellous record of the British landscape in the 1940s (a benchmark from which to assess the impact of intensive farming and landscape change in more recent years). This survey also recorded sites of archaeological significance. Photographs were taken at regular intervals along transect routes and record a vertical rather than oblique view. There is usually an overlap with the adjacent photographs allowing the use of stereoscopic glasses to obtain a three-dimensional view of the landscape. This is particularly useful in identifying landforms, although the oblique view taken in low sunlight can reveal more subtle changes in relief.

The detection of sites by aerial photography is due to a number of soil and vegetation characteristics, such as shadow marks, crop marks, and soil marks. Shadow marks are observed when the low sunlight emphasises irregularities in the ground surface by highlighting bumps and filling hollows with shadow. Crop marks are created when buried features cause a reduction or enhancement of crop growth through their moisture retention properties. Crop marks are mostly likely to be revealed during drought conditions. Soil marks are observed when the land has been ploughed, causing building fragments to be brought near to the surface which give variations in soil colour.

18 Trimworth Downs, 1973.

This vertical aerial photograph, taken in June 1973, shows Trimworth in the top left quadrant, marked with a black square. Godmersham Park lies in the top right quadrant. When compared with recent O.S. maps at a similar scale, it is possible to appreciate the landscape change which has taken place under the influence of intensive farming. (© NMR)

Results and interpretation for Trimworth

Photographs obtained from the National Monuments Records (English Heritage) provide good evidence of former activity back to the Iron Age. They can also be used to obtain a record of landscape change occurring over the last 50 years. Particularly striking is the evidence of early agricultural activity dating from the Iron Age, although some may date from Saxon or early medieval periods. Fig. 13 represents the farmed landscape of Godmersham Park (TR057508), with tracks, field boundaries and plough markings as they were in 1979 when the photograph was taken. However, half-hidden beneath this modern farmed landscape is the evidence of earlier field boundaries shown in crop and soil markings. They are rectangular in shape, measuring 40 to 60 metres across, surviving on the relatively dry, smooth chalk soils. Cultivation of these fields was probably abandoned when farmers moved to lower slopes and the heavier, more fertile soils of the Stour Valley, but aerial photography has revealed this distant period of our history embedded in the landscape despite several hundred years of subsequent cultivation.

Other aerial photographs of Trimworth Downs, across the river from these old farmed landscapes, reveal the extent of landscape change occurring in recent generations. A series of RAF photographs taken just after the Second World War can be compared with recent Ordnance Survey maps to monitor changes in the rural landscape resulting from intensive cultivation. These changes include the removal of field boundaries, increasing field sizes, alterations of margins separating farmed and non-farmed land, fluctuation of woodland cover, alteration of tracks, removal, addition, extension of farm buildings, etc. (Fig. 18).

Availability of sources of aerial photography

The National Monuments Records Centre at Swindon holds the largest reference collection of aerial photographs in England, totalling around four million. They provide a unique coverage of the country from the earliest days of flying to the present day. The specialist collection of over 600,000 oblique air photographs is predominantly of archaeological, architectural and landscape subjects dating from the 1930s to the present day. The three million vertical air photographs comprise a national coverage taken by the RAF in the 1940s, supplemented by commercial sources as follows:

1. RAF 1940 to 1965, including 1946/7 national survey at a 1:10,000 scale.

2. Ordnance Survey 1952 to 1979, 1:5,000 to 1:23,000.

3. Meridian Air Maps 1952 to 1984, 1:3,000 to 1:30,000

To use the facility of the NMR, it is best to obtain a form which allows you to request a search. The information required for a search is the place-name and grid reference of the site, and a recommended radius up to a maximum of nine km² over which the search should be made. For example, the request for Trimworth was made for a radius of 300 metres, from which 40 vertical photographs were identified. The standard searches are undertaken within 15 working days, and a priority search within two days. The information you will receive is in the form of a database of the photographs held for the area requested and is free of charge. This database records information on the quality of the image, scale and date of sortie, etc. Having decided which images are required, a request for photocopies or laser copies can be made. If you visit the NMR, it is possible to undertake your own search. (Details of how to contact the NMR are given at the end of the previous section on Sources for Archaeology.)

This chapter has reviewed the importance of the landscape in revealing evidence of former settlements and sites of economic activity. It has also identified important factors influencing the site and situation of the house, such as the local geology, river patterns, relief and soils, and previous settlement histories. This broad-ranging survey is now followed by a closer focus on the house itself, through an examination of architectural history.

Chapter 4

The House as a Document

Research on the physical structure of the house can reveal vital information on the age of the house, the way in which it was built, and the materials used, all of which form background to later documentary searches. There are regional building styles with which you will become familiar, allowing you to date your house. In the South East, the variety of building material (wood, bricks, sandstone, flint, etc.) has led to a variety of styles, but the vernacular form most commonly found is the Wealden hall house, of which Trimworth is an example.

There are many books and other sources on different types of houses which will help you to date your house, such as **www.lookingatbuildings.org.uk**. This is a joint venture between Pevsner Architectural Guides and the Buildings Book Trust, and includes good material on regional building variations and construction methods, with photographs and a glossary. (For a fascinating insight into how social change through history has influenced building styles, see **www.bricksandbrass. co.uk**.) The Pevsner Architectural Guides themselves are a wonderful source. In 1951, Sir Nicholas Pevsner, an architectural historian, began to produce up-to-date portable guides to the most significant buildings throughout the British Isles. Each volume contains an overview of the architectural history of the area, and a descriptive gazetteer arranged alphabetically by place. The volume *Kent: West and the Weald* features great country houses and also domestic buildings of all periods. Although your house may not be included, a great deal can be learned about architectural styles which relate to your home.

The Architectural History of Trimworth Manor

The author cannot claim to have expertise in the constructional techniques of medieval domestic buildings. This section therefore focuses on two major sources; firstly, the series of books by the Royal Commission on Historical Monuments resulting from a survey on medieval rural houses in Kent. *The House Within: Interpreting Medieval Houses in Kent* gives details of layout, structure and building form. The companion volume, *The Medieval Houses of Kent; An Historical Analysis*, examines the great variety in form, numbers and distribution of medieval properties across the county. Both books are supported by a gazetteer of medieval houses in Kent. These sources have made it possible to chart the evolution of Trimworth and draw attention to features and fragments of interest. The second source is an architectural description of

19 Stone fragments, Trimworth.
Carved stone, possibly representing window tracery and door post, found near the present house. Could these be ruins of a former house, or the chapel associated with Trimworth?

Trimworth Manor undertaken by Rupert Austin of the Canterbury Archaeological Trust in April 2005. This brief archaeological inspection provided a valuable insight into the long and complex history of the house.

The origins of the house date back to before the Norman Conquest. A charter of the year 824 refers to a fishpond at 'dreaman wyrthe' (Trimworth), but the fabric that survives today is not of such antiquity. The present structure started life, perhaps, in the late 15th century, as a timber-framed open-hall house, although interesting fragments of stone from an earlier domestic or ecclesiastical building have been found around the existing building (Fig. 19). No medieval house survives intact; all have been altered to a greater or lesser extent, and Trimworth has experienced considerable modification. Nevertheless, it displays many features of the original medieval fabric. The frontage of the house comprises three distinct elements aligned north to south. The central element stands where the former open hall was located; this part of the building is

20 Trimworth Manor, east-facing aspect.
Note the modifications to the original open-hall house (raised roof line, addition of Jacobean porch, etc.).

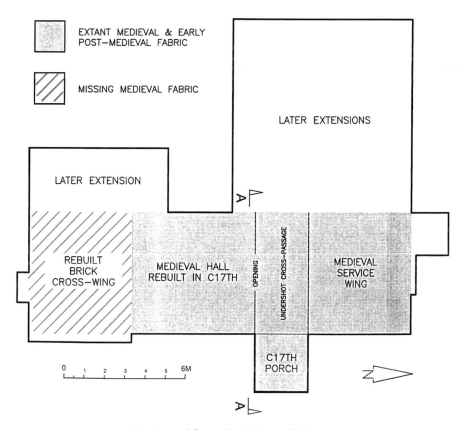

EXTANT MEDIEVAL & EARLY
POST–MEDIEVAL FABRIC

MISSING MEDIEVAL FABRIC

LATER EXTENSIONS

LATER EXTENSION

REBUILT
BRICK
CROSS–WING

MEDIEVAL HALL
REBUILT IN C17TH

OPENING

UNDERSHOT CROSS–PASSAGE

MEDIEVAL
SERVICE
WING

0 1 2 3 4 5 6M

C17TH
PORCH

21   Ground-floor plan, Trimworth Manor.

easily distinguished because it is taller than the rest (Fig. 20). The medieval service wing survives to the north of the former hall, and is now fronted by a 17th-century porch. A brick cross-wing lies to the south, where the former high end of the medieval house once stood. More recent east-to-west aligned brick buildings lie to the rear of the property, as shown on the ground-floor plan (Fig. 21).

Basic elements of the open-hall house

Kent has an extraordinarily rich heritage of timber-framed houses, possibly more than any other English county. They cover a wide social spectrum from the wealthiest elements of society (including those of ecclesiastical institutions such as Canterbury Cathedral) to the tenant farmer. One of the finest can be seen at the Weald and Downland Open Air Museum at Singleton near Chichester. 'Bayleaf' was presented to the museum by the East Surrey Water Company prior to the creation of the Bough Beech reservoir. The building has been reconstructed without subsequent modifications or alterations, and stands as it was first built in the early 15th century. A fundamental feature of all hall houses is the hall itself, which generally occupied the area from the ground floor up to the underside of the roof. The open hall was heated by

22   Soot-blackened beams.

a) (above) The north wall of the old hall house with blackened lath and daub. The roof apex of the old hall can be seen a metre below the existing roof apex.

b) (below) Blackened rafters beneath a more recently constructed Kent-peg tiled roof.

a fire in the centre of the room, with the smoke rising to the roof. Without a chimney to channel the smoke, the roof space became blackened, and this feature is often a key indication that a subsequently altered building once contained an open hall. The lath and daub in the roof-space at Trimworth is blackened with a hard coating of granular, sooty material (Fig. 22). There are also many soot-blackened rafters, although it is unwise to assume hall status on this feature alone, because many old houses suffered fire damage in more recent times. It seems likely that the open hall at Trimworth was located in the centre of the house, and was two bays in length. All that now survives is the east-west aligned cross-frame that formed its north wall.

This frame is clearly visible from the entrance hall and main stairway, and is typically constructed of a substantial cambered tie-beam supported by jowled posts. Long curved down-braces descend from the posts to the first-floor bridging-beam (Figs 23 and 24). A crown post sits on top of the tie-beam, revealing the roof form that covered the hall. The crown posts of the service wing also survive. The frame reveals the hall to have been approximately 8.1 metres high from ground floor to ridge, and approximately 5.4 metres wide.

The position of a one-metre opening into the service wing is revealed by large square mortices in the first-floor bridging beam in the entrance hall. A third square mortice for a later inserted post lies within the centre of this opening. Presumably the opening was later blocked up and replaced by a door at the western end of the partition. Evidence for this newer entrance is shown in the wear pattern on the brick floor. It is likely that the opening described here would have led into the low-end or service wing of the house, because the high-end of the hall typically had a dais bench, above which was an elaborately moulded bridging beam. (This may survive, buried in the wall of the ground-floor dining room.)

A cross-passage was usually located at the service wing end of a medieval hall, with the front and rear doors of the house at either end of the passage. Service

23   North wall of the hall house.
a) (left) Showing the tie beam, curved down-braces and jowled posts, infilled with lath and daub.
b) (right) View from the cross-passage on ground floor looking up the north wall to the substantial cambered tie beam.

wings usually accommodated two ground-floor rooms, the buttery and the pantry, accessed through two doors leading off the cross-passage. There is no evidence for these doors in the cross-frame at Trimworth, just a single wide opening, suggesting therefore that Trimworth probably contained an undershot passage which lay immediately adjacent to the hall, within the service wing itself. Further evidence that Trimworth Manor contained an undershot passage is confirmed by the location of the 17th-century porch, which lies in front of the passage position. Although it is a later addition, this porch seems to maintain the original point of access into the building, replacing the original front door.

Rebuilding the hall

By the end of the 15th century, open halls had become unfashionable. Gradually, the basic plan of the hall evolved to suit changing social and economic needs. Smoke bays, timber or brick chimneys and fireplaces, and new ceilings were added to create more and better accommodation. This was not always a gradual systematic evolution; at Trimworth the older open hall was virtually demolished and rebuilt rather than gradually modified. That such wholesale rebuilding occurred is perhaps indicative of the

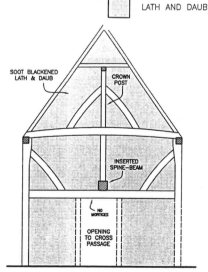

LATH AND DAUB

SOOT BLACKENED LATH & DAUB

CROWN POST

INSERTED SPINE–BEAM

NO MORTICES

OPENING TO CROSS PASSAGE

24   Section of north wall of hall house.
The location of the section A-A is shown in Fig. 21. Note the structural elements of the timbers, shown in Fig. 23.

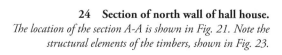

SECTION A - A, LOOKING NORTH

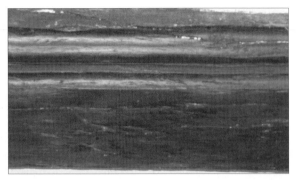

25   Beam mouldings.
Seventeenth-century alterations include carved beams to support ceilings in what was the old open hall.

wealth of the owners, who presumably had the financial means to undertake major alterations while others had to make do with modest adjustments to the existing structure over a longer period of time.

Modifying the existing hall was not an ideal solution, because halls were typically less than two full storeys in height, so newly inserted floors often meant that upper rooms extended into the roof space. By completely rebuilding the hall, the owners at Trimworth avoided this problem. The new structure, probably built in the early 17th century, seems to have occupied the same footprint as the old hall, its length and width remaining unchanged. However, it was rebuilt to a full two-storey height, the ridge now being 90 cm higher than that of the service wing, giving generous head room. The former old hall now had single ground- and first-floor rooms, together with a ground-floor hall.

The first-floor beams of the rebuilt hall are clearly visible from the hall and dining room. They are decorated with cyma and cavetto mouldings. Cavetto is a diminutive of cavo, meaning hollow, so named because it is a concave moulding with a cross-section approximating a quarter-circle. Cyma is a moulding with the upper section concave and the lower section convex (Fig. 25). Both mouldings are typical of the 17th century. The

26   Crown post.
(Above) Located above the service wing. The plain square post was braced on all four sides, only the north/south braces remain to meet the collar purlin.

27   Roof rafters.
Note contrast between medieval rafters, laid flat, (5.5in x 3in) and more recent square rafters.

28 Floorboards.
The wide oak floor boards in the existing bedroom are certainly early, probably original.

29 Coats of arms.
(Left) Kempe family, three wheat sheaves; (right) Kempe and Argall families combined, three wheat sheaves, three lions' heads.

common joists are plainly chamfered indicating that they were intended to be seen. None of the tie-beams show any evidence of partitions, confirming that a single room occupied the ground floor of the new structure. None of the original windows survive, however an ovolo-moulded window-head, with mortices for the missing mullions, can be seen at the north end of rebuilt hall within the roof of the later extension. The roof of the rebuilt hall is a simple collar-rafter form rather than a crown post construction. Many of the rafters are soot-blackened and have probably been reused from the old hall roof.

The service wing

The service wing is the only part of the original medieval house that now survives. It is two bays in length (approximately 22ft), aligned with the hall, which is unusual because most

30 Jacobean porch.
Probably built shortly after the arrival of Sir Reginald Kempe in 1607, it was originally timber-framed, now underpinned with red brick, laid in Flemish bond.

31   Box framing in porch chamber.
Small, square framing constructed using a mid-rail, in the style of the 17th century.

32   16th-century Flemish floor tiles.
These green-glazed floor tiles (six inches square, one inch thick) were found in the area of the cross-passage about eight inches below the existing floor.

bay wings are aligned at right-angles to the main hall. A two-bay crown-post survives over the service wing. The post is plain, square, and was braced on all four sides, although only the north-south braces survive to meet the collar purlin (Fig. 26). The rafters measure an average 14cm by 8cm and are laid flat in a medieval manner (Fig. 27). No partition appears to have been present on either side of the central crown-post, suggesting that a single chamber occupied the first floor of the wing. This chamber would have been open to the roof. The wide oak floorboards in the existing bedroom are certainly early, and probably original (Fig. 28).

The 17th-century porch

An attractive two-storey porch was added against the front wall of the service wing in the early 17th century (Fig. 29). This was probably all timber-framed, but is now underpinned at ground level with red brick laid in Flemish bond. The first-floor elevations have been rendered externally. Unusual brackets lie beneath the jettied gable of the porch in which grotesque characters carry the arms of Sir Reginald Kempe on the left bracket (three wheat sheaves), and of his wife Mary, daughter of Richard Argall of East Sutton, on the right (three wheat sheaves and three lions' heads) (Fig. 30). Above the brackets rise the barge-boards, attractively carved and pierced. An oriel window with ovolo-moulded mullions lies beneath the jettied gable. A Jacobean door-frame leads from the upper-storey chamber of the porch into the main bedroom. Small square framing can be seen within the porch chamber, constructed using a mid-rail in the style of the 17th century (Fig. 31). Recent work in the hallway just outside the porch door revealed at least one level of tiled flooring. Samples of tiles were inspected by the Canterbury Archaeological Trust, and their report suggests Flemish glazed floor tiles from the 15th to early 16th centuries. This type of tile was manufactured over a 200-year period from 1350 and generally decreased in size from the medieval to post-medieval period. The Trimworth tiles are six inches wide and 1.2in thick, dating them to a later period of manufacture (mid-16th century) (Fig. 32). Several tiles had a green glaze on an underlying white slip, the latter facilitating adherence of the glaze and also illuminating the colour. This type of tile, made in yellow, brown and green glazes, was used in a variety of buildings from domestic buildings to friaries, priories and churches. They were laid in a variety of patterns, a chequered pattern being most common. One example of an excavation that produced a large number of these tiles was situated in Northgate Canterbury (the site of the student residence at Lanfranc). This was the site of a medieval priory.

Conclusion

The present building appears to have started life as a medieval hall-house, which was substantially rebuilt in the early 17th century, although a two-bay service wing to the north of the former hall still survives from the 15th century. It seems reasonable to suggest that Sir Reginald Kempe, who acquired the property in 1607, instigated much of the rebuilding. Certainly, the porch is attributable to him, for it bears his own arms. Further alterations were made in the 18th century, when brick replaced much of the timber-frame. Additions in the early 19th century were added at the rear of the building, which would have doubled the size of the original hall-house.

Various authors have noted the removal of important architectural items from the house. Igglesden's series of *Saunters through Kent*, written in 1939, refers to 'wainscotting carved with the arms of Kempe, and the explanation of its disappearance is that much of the panelling was sold to an American who, about 50 years ago, bought up other carving in the Tudor buildings of the neighbourhood'. Not all items travelled so far. An article by C.R. Councer on painted glass in Wye College (*Archaeologia Cantiana*, 1985, vol. 102, p.225) notes the removal of stained glass from 'Tremworth'. The removal is recorded in the memoirs of the Revd Phillip Parsons, curate of Wye, in which he writes, 'I have recovered the arms of the founder [i.e. Archbishop Kempe], from a neighboring farmhouse, [Tremworth] … and inserted them with additional ornaments in a window of the front hall.' (*Monuments and Painted Glass of Upwards of 100 Churches*, pp.10-12.) There are no plans yet to recover this glass and reinstate it where it rightfully belongs – Trimworth Manor!

The story of Trimworth has demonstrated the value of using the house's structure as a way of tracing its history. The structural styles, decorative and architectural features give important clues about the period in which it was constructed. However, over-reliance on architectural evidence has its pitfalls. An untrained eye may attribute an early construction date to a rebuild in a retrospective style, or one that used salvaged materials from older houses. For these and other reasons, architectural evidence should be combined with evidence from early written records. These will be examined in the next chapter.

CHAPTER 5

Early Written Records

PLACE-NAMES: SIGNPOSTS TO THE PAST

Not only is the study of place-names fascinating, it also provides historical value. They remain as a word-map of the distant past, an index of history, as signposts to earlier settlement. They illustrate the contribution that individuals and families have made to the societies of their time, as well as providing evidence of topographical features in the landscape, using a vocabulary to express subtle distinctions in the lie of the land. They occasionally refer to vegetation in the landscape, such as forest, marsh, or open country, which has long since been engulfed by urban growth or incursions of the sea. The interpretation of place-names requires caution. It is often difficult to assess the age of a settlement by its place-name, because an incoming group of people may have colonised an area, changing previous place-names to suit their own linguistic forms. Another general problem that confronts the interpreter is the extent to which we can interpret the first element of a place-name as a personal name. However, despite these notes of caution, the study of place-names in relation to the study of settlements, houses and landforms is extremely rewarding, especially when placed alongside supporting archaeological and documentary evidence. Following an overview of the county of Kent, the place and house names in the parish of Crundale will be examined, before taking Trimworth Manor as a specific case study.

In 55 and 54 B.C. Caesar penetrated into Kent, adopting the old British word 'Cantium' (from *canto*, meaning rim or edge), a name which has changed only slightly over the centuries, making Kent the oldest county name in Britain. Apart from a small number of rivers and coastal features, names of settlements of Celtic origin have nearly all disappeared. We have Dover (from *dubro*, meaning water or river), Edenbridge (from *eadhelms bridge*), Sheerness (from *scir*, meaning bright, pure, clear, as in bright headland), and finally Lenham (from *leands ham*). It is likely that the incoming Romans latinised the existing British forms they found here. Scandinavian evidence is virtually absent, but the Saxons stamped their impression firmly on the landscape, settling the conquered territory to make a rich, well-organised kingdom. It is the Saxons whose names are the true foundation of the place-names of Kent, whether towns, villages, hamlets, farms, houses, woods, hills or streams. It was during the earliest phase of settlement from about A.D. 450 that most place-names ending in *-ing* or *-ingas* (meaning farm) first come into use. Sometimes these are prefixed by personal names or landscape features. Of equal antiquity are the

-ham (meaning homestead, dwelling, house, hamlet or manor) or *-hamm* (meaning enclosure, meadow, water meadow) endings, probably related to the verb 'to hem' or enclose within a border, just as water meadows were enclosed to protect crops or animals in the Saxon economy. Of a similar period is the ending *-ge* (meaning district), such as Lyminge, a district in the River Lympne, and *-ware* (dwellers), as in *Cantwaraburgh* (fortress or city of the Kent dwellers). This is the earliest form of the place name for Canterbury. Another example is *Tenetwaradenn* (Tenterden). This means 'swine pasture of the Men of Thanet', suggesting the economic importance of swine herding on the edge of oak forests to exploit the acorn harvest, which in this case meant a link with a Wealden settlement forty miles away. Other place-names incorporate the names of ancient tribes or heathen beliefs, as in *-wig*, meaning a pagan idol or shrine. (The term 'pagan' here is to denote pre-Christian religious beliefs, covering Celtic, Roman and Anglo-Saxon cultures.)

In Anglo-Saxon England almost every landscape feature, whether natural or man-made, had a name, such as a hill name (*dun*), valley names (*dalr* and *dael*), as in Crundale or Deal, marsh names (*mere*), woodlands (*wold*), tree names, such as the ash (*aesc*) as in Ashford, or more fully described as *aesc – sceat – ford* (ford by the corner of land where ash trees grow). Words for tracks, roads and paths were also common, as were buildings and dwellings. In fact, one of the commonest elements is *tun*, meaning 'that which is enclosed', often used in combination with a personal name.

Finally, the importance of agriculture in the Saxon economy is inevitably reflected in place-names, whether for crops (as in *bere*, or *baer* meaning barley), types of enclosure (*tun*, *worth*, *croft*) or soil types, as in 'Sandwich' or 'Chart', *chert* being a type of flint stone, although sometimes the word *ceart* denotes rough ground.

Place-names in the parish of Crundale

The settlement of Crundale appears in documents in various forms, initially Crundala (1100, *Domesday Monachorum*) then Crumdal (1226), Crumdale (1226), Crudale (1226) and Crundale (1242). All forms probably derive from the old English *crundel* meaning ravine, chalk pit, quarry, or *crumb* (cooked) and *dell* (dell, hollow, valley, dale). Within Crundale village is Denwood or Danord Street, from the old English *denu* meaning dale or valley, plus a ford.

To the north of Sole Street lies Barton Wood, formerly known as Bertone, Bartone, Bertume, Berton, all of which derive from the old English *beretun,* meaning 'Barley farm'. Sole Street itself probably comes from the old English *Sol*, meaning 'muddy pool'. There is an old dewpond (*sol*) situated at 485 feet on the edge of the flat top of the high downs in the north-east corner of the parish. The name Hessole Street probably has a similar origin, from the old English *heorot,* meaning 'hart' plus 'sol', meaning muddy pool.

The names of other woodlands in the parish have interesting origins. Fanscoombe Wood derives from *fen, fenn* and *cumb,* 'valley'. Vineys Wood, which lies east of

Crundale, originated as *deffinegh*, from the Old English *fin* plus *hege*, meaning an enclosure, although an alternative origin could be the old English *fin* meaning hill or hilly woodland. Purr Wood (*Pur wuda*) is an ancient woodland close to Trimworth. The word *pur* is probably a derivation of 'clean, pure,' meaning an unbroken or undisturbed wood. Farms close to Trimworth are also interesting. Ripple Farm derives from the old English *rippel*, meaning 'a strip of land'. Winchcombe Farm has a number of early forms, including Wincelcumbe (825) and de Wynchecombe (1200). The common meaning of all terms is from the old English *wincel*, meaning 'corner or angle', and *cumbe*, meaning 'valley'. Hunt Street Farm takes its name from a family named *Hunte*, which had been resident in Crundale since the early 14th century. At one time, this property belonged to the manor of Cakes Yoke, which lies a short distance further down the lane. A yoke was about 60 acres, and in 1312 John Cake held the two yokes jointly. Marriage Farm is on the boundary of Wye and Crundale, and the name probably derives from the Old English *gemaere*, meaning 'border or boundary', and *hrycg*, meaning 'ridge'. Olantigh, which adjoins Trimworth, is derived from *hole(g)n*, meaning 'holly', and *teag*, 'enclosure'. Nearby, Buckwell Farm probably originated as Berchvelle (1086), and is derived from *boc*, meaning 'beech tree', and *welle*, 'a spring or well'. Hurst Farm, on the boundary between Chilham and Godmersham, is derived from the Old English *hyrst* meaning 'a wood, a hill' or 'a wood on a hill'.

The origins of the name 'Trimworth'

Trimworth is first recorded in an Anglo-Saxon charter of 824 as *dreaman wyrthe*, and subsequently occurs in many forms, such as Dreamwurthe (1100), Dreingworth (1207), Tremewrth (1218), Tremesworth (1237), de Trenworth (1240), Thremworthe (1242), Tremworth (1254) and, more recently, Trimworth.

The origins of the name come from the Old English *dreama*, meaning 'joy, delight, mirth', and *worth*, meaning 'enclosure'. Researchers of place-names suggest that *worth* is commonly combined with a personal name or a personal quality, as in this case, where the characteristic would be one of a happy, joyful person.

Additional sources for further and more detailed study of place-names can be found in the list of references for Chapter 5.

ANGLO-SAXON ESTATE BOUNDARIES OR CARTULARIES

One of the great sources in the study of the obscure and distant Anglo-Saxon period is the **Land Charter**, which refers to the estates of individuals or monastic institutions. Hundreds of land charters survive from the late seventh century onwards, which set out the boundaries of the estate, right down to a single tree, a bank, a bend in the river, or an old building. Tracing the route of an Anglo-Saxon Charter in the field is an exciting and rewarding exercise, as the great local historian W.G. Hoskins powerfully recognised.

> This exercise gives one a truer and more detailed knowledge of the English countryside than any other pursuit not excluding fox hunting. By the time one

has scrambled over hedges, leapt across boggy streams in deep woods, traversed narrow green lanes all but blocked with brambles and the luxuriant vegetation of wet summers, not to mention to have walked upon high airy ridges on a day of tumultuous blue and white skies with magnificent views of deep country all around – by the time one has done this, armed with a copy of a Saxon Charter and the two and half inch maps, the topography of some few miles of the English landscape is indelibly printed on the mind and heart. And at the same time, one has the constant intellectual exercise of fitting the frequently obscure landmarks of the Charter to the ground one is traversing, and the mental excitement of making some unmistakable identification and of revealing to oneself the age of some ordinary feature of the scene – a ditch, a hedge, a piece of marsh, a pond, or what you will.

(W.G. Hoskins, *The Making of the English Landscape*, Pelican (1955), pp. 66-7)

Identifying the route of a recorded estate boundary in the field is therefore fascinating field work, establishing a link with the landscape features which existed over 1,100 years ago. The only requirement is an Ordnance Survey map (1:25,000), which can be related at a later stage to the 1:10,000 map for greater detail. However the task is not so straightforward in practice. Although all the boundary points follow in logical order, each being related to the one before and after, there will inevitably be some confusion. It is a slow process with constant cross-referencing between map and field. Often older maps will provide some clues, for example the tithe map will show older boundaries that survive today and record field names which have long since passed out of use. Estate maps of the 17th and 18th centuries are invaluable for similar reasons. A vital clue in this work is often the parish boundary, which generally coincides with the Charter boundary for much of its length. Caution is needed here, because the original ecclesiastical parish boundary may not coincide with the civil parish boundary. In the latter part of the 19th century there was a good deal of 'tidying up' of anomalies, nevertheless the correspondence between the estate boundary and the parish boundary is often close. In the end, the exercise of combining the written document with the field work is rewarding and fascinating. As Hoskins so aptly puts it, 'Once the Charter is "solved", one has the intellectual satisfaction akin to that of a mathematician who has solved a long and difficult equation.' (Hoskins, *op. cit.*, p.39.)

Trimworth and the Anglo-Saxon Charter

The estate boundary of greatest relevance here is that for *Godmeares Ham* (Godmersham), dating from 824, in which Trimworth Manor appears for the first time in written record. The original parchment document, held in the Manuscript Room of the British Library, measures 30 ins by 9 ins. It is quite fragile, but the script is clearly legible. The document is a record of proceedings held in 824 at the Synod of Clovesho under the presidency of Beornwulf, King of the Mercians (who died in battle a year later). It involves a dispute over land on an estate at Oeswal (Eastwell?)

33 Anglo-Saxon Charter, 824.

a) Godmersham and Challock 'land marks'.

The main document relates to the resolution of a land dispute. On the reverse of the parchment document, some ancient archivist of Christ Church Canterbury (?) has set out the boundaries of Godmersham and Challock. The end of the second line refers to 'dreamen wurthe' (Trimworth). (© British Library Board. All rights reserved. Stowe Charter 14, side 2.)

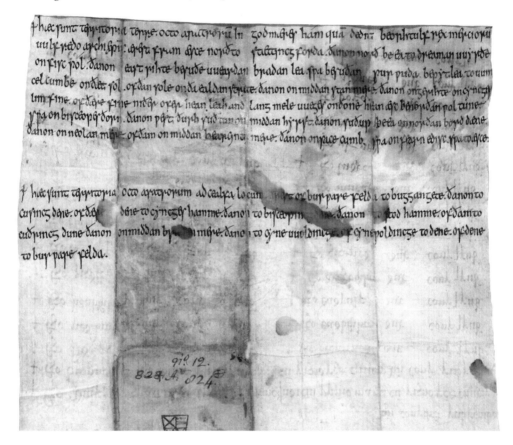

b) Translation of the Godmersham and Challock 'land marks'.

These are the landmarks of the eight ploughs in Godmersham which Beorhtwulf, King of Mercians, has given to Archbishop Wulfred. First from Ash North to Straetineg ford; thence north by river to Dreamen wurthe in Fish pool; thence east straight by southward of Broad lea; so south of Purwood by Pytlea to Winchelcombe on the Sole; from the Sole to the old street; thence to Mid Stanmere' thence straight on to the King's lime heap; from the heap down over Heanlea along Meda way to the high ash north of Woltune; so to Bishop's thorn; thence west through Sutton to Mid hyrst; thence south by river to Borddean; thence to Deep mere; from Mid Hearcineges mere; thence to Saccombe; so to Fern stuubble; so to ash.

These are the landmarks of the eight ploughs at Challock. First from Burgess field to Buckgate; thence to Cosinegdene; from the dene to Kingsham; thence to Bishopingdene; thence to Stodham; from that to Cuthrineg down; thence to the middle of Broad mere; thence to Cynewoldineg; from Cynewoldineg to Dene; from Dene to Burgess field.

34 Boundary map of the Charter of 824.

The route corresponds closely with the present parish boundary, some is on public footpaths but much cuts across fields with no right of way. Figs 35 to 40 illustrate the characteristics of the route and some prominent landscape features.

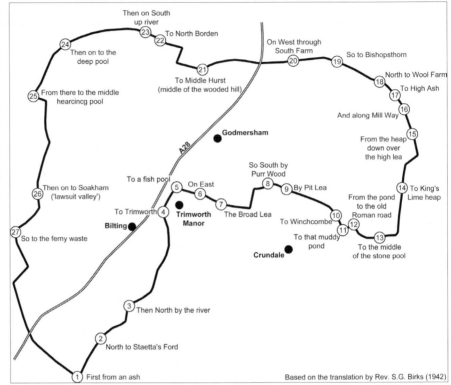

which had been bequeathed to Archbishop Wulfred by Earl Aldberht and his sister the abbess of Selethryth and unjustly held from him by Quenthyrth, abbess of Selemynstre (minister of Thanet). The document restores the estate to Archbishop Wulfred and is witnessed by the Archbishop himself, King Beornwulf, nine bishops, two abbots, two priest abbots, 13 dukes and a footman. On the reverse of this record is set out the boundaries of two estates, one at *Godmeares Ham* (Godmersham), the other at *Cealfaloc* (Challock). A copy of this original document is produced in Fig. 33a, and the translation of these 11 lines of clearly written Old English text is seen in Fig. 33b. The approximate location of the Godmersham boundary is shown in Fig. 34. The route has recently been walked and coincides closely with the present parish boundary of Godmersham. Illustrations of relevant features along the route are shown in Figs 35 to 40.

Sources of Anglo-Saxon land charters

As far as is known, there is no up-to-date inventory of charters for the country as a whole. Many counties are covered in the three-volume work, *Studies in early English History,* published by Leicester University Press. H.B.R. Finberg's *Early Charters of the West Midlands* (1961) lists the charters for Gloucestershire, Worcestershire, Herefordshire and Shropshire. Finberg has also published *Early Charters of Wessex*

35 'North to Staettincgforda' (north to the ford called after Staetta).
This is probably the site of the present Sparrows Bridge, shown here. This shows the original course of the Stour. In 1846 a straight cut was constructed to eliminate the need for two railway bridges being built over the old river, which is now a backwater.

36 'To dreaman uuyrthe on fisc pol' (to Trimworth into the fish pool).
Located just to the north of Trimworth where the Stour meanders and deepens on the outside curve of the river.

37 'Swa be suthan pur wuda be pytlea to uuincelcumbe' (so on by south part of Purr Wood by the pit clearing as far as Winchcombe).
This picture shows Winchcombe (meaning a corner or angle in the valley) with Purr Wood in the distance, an ancient woodland whose name is probably derived from pure, clean (i.e. unbroken, undisturbed).

**38 'thanon west thurh suth tun on middan hyrst'
(then west through the south farm in the middle of
the wooded hill).**
*This location is where the boundary crosses the Stour west
of Hurst Farm.*

39   Kings Wood.
*Another ancient woodland of beech, sweet chestnut,
corsican pine and Douglas fir, through which the
boundary runs for nearly three miles.*

(1964), covering Hampshire, Wiltshire, Somerset and Dorset, and covered the counties
of Devon and Cornwall in 'Early Charters of Devon and Cornwall' (*Occasional
Paper 2*, Leicester University Press, revised 1963).

C.R. Hart's *Early Charters of Eastern England* deals with Huntingdonshire,
Cambridgeshire, Norfolk, Suffolk, Lincolnshire, Rutland, and the Soke of
Peterborough. The county of Essex has also been published by Hart in *Early Charters of
Essex,* published by Leicester University Press (*Occasional Papers 10 and 11, 1957*).

Facsimiles of charters can be found in W.B. Sanders, *Facsimiles of Anglo-Saxon
Manuscripts*, 3 vols (Ordnance Survey), 1878-84. The Godmersham charter is vol. 3,
no. 17. All three volumes are held at the British Library Manuscript Room under the
reference 1777d5.

See also W. de Gray Birch, *Cartularium Saxonicum*, 3 vols, 1885-99.

The Godmersham charter is discussed by Patricia Winzar in 'An Anglo-Saxon
Perambulation', *Journal of Kent History,* March 2002.

DOMESDAY BOOK

'Domesday Book is unique. A survey of England made in 1086/87, it is unmatched in
its age, its scope and its consistent details of its contents … an endlessly rich source of
historical material.' Thus begins the introduction to *The Domesday Book, a Complete
Translation*, by Williams and Martin (Penguin Classics, 2002).

The Domesday survey was commissioned by William the Conqueror in 1085 and thereby carried royal authority in its compilation. It is considered to be the work of one person. The completed survey gave an account of the disposition of wealth and power over the 20 years since the conquest. It recorded the resources held by individual manors (landholdings, equipment), and assessed the overall value of each, and it enables a picture of the population distribution to be envisaged, although this was not its primary purpose. 'It produced an astonishing result; a complex return of the resources of the land, and their division between the King and the Lords to whom he granted them, based on testimony.' (Williams and Martin, *op. cit.*, page vii.) Its name, Domesday, 'The book of the day of Judgement', suggests the awe in which the book was held.

Domesday Kent

Domesday Book opens with a description of Kent and its division into lathes, an intermediate administrative unit between the county and the hundred. The lathe originated as a unit of the Jutish Kingdom of Kent, each with its *villa regalis* at the centre and a share of the Wealden forest. The lathe first appeared in documents of the sixth century. Domesday mentions seven lathes for Kent, of which one is Wye, running in a wide swathe across East Kent from the coast of Sheppey to Hawkhurst on the Sussex border. Its size is clear evidence of its importance. Each lathe is divided into hundreds; somewhat confusingly the Wye lathe contains nine hundreds, one of which is called Wye. The manorial data in Kent Domesday is usually set out in five standard recurring items: sulungs, plough lands, plough teams, population, and values. The sulung is a unit of assessment equivalent to two hides (notionally the amount of land which will support a household). In some cases, the term yoke is also used which is the equivalent of one quarter of a sulung. Oxon were yoked in pairs, and a full plough team would have consisted of four pairs of oxen. The estimate of the arable capacity of an estate in terms of the number of eight-ox plough teams needed to work it was measured in plough lands. Frequently a discrepancy arises in

40 'thanon on sacecumb' (then on to Soakham).

The farm of this name is probably derived from the old English 'sacu', meaning conflict or dispute or lawsuit. Presumably, the possession of the valley and the farm was in dispute.

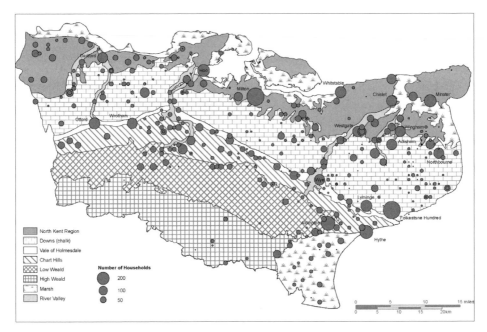

41   Domesday Kent, population distribution by household.
The map has been constructed for the 350 or so manorial units, with circles proportionate to size of community. Note the string of manors along the Stour Valley from Wye to Canterbury, including Trimworth. (From An Historical Atlas of Kent, *Phillimore, 2004).*

the relationship between plough land and plough teams. For example, at Wye there were 52 plough lands, but only 26 teams were at work, whereas in the manor of Norton (Whitstable) there were 66½ plough teams recorded, but only 26 plough lands. The number of plough lands in Kent amounted to over 3,150 in total.

Domesday Book was not meant to be a census of population, although it is possible to arrive at a reasonable estimate. The bulk of the population was divided into villeins (an unfree peasant villager), bordars (a cottager of lower socio-economic status than a villein), and others, including slaves. Campbell, in her *Domesday Geography of South East England*, arrives at a figure for the county of 11,753 *men* (of which 6,800 were villeins and 3,400 bordars), but this figure must be increased to obtain an estimated population of fifty thousand. To this must be added the urban populations, priests and canons, bringing the total to about seventy thousand. Figure 41 gives an impression of their location in the manorial units.

The value of the estates was measured in pounds and given for three dates; firstly 1066, secondly the year in which the holder received the estate, and thirdly for 1086. Figures show increases and decreases in value over this period of time, the decreases often being the result of devastation caused by the passage of Norman armies. The Domesday entry for Dover, for example, notes that the borough had been burnt down and could not be properly valued. Many villages around Dover and in East Kent were similarly affected, although most had recovered by 1096. The value of Trimworth was recorded as £10 in 1066, falling to £7, and then recovering to over £14 by 1086.

Other entries in Domesday Book which provide details of the economic geography of the county include woodlands, which were recorded in terms of the number of swine paid to the lord for the right of pannage. Many estates owned swine pastures in the Weald, despite being some distance away. These pastures were called denns or denes, and were connected to the villages by droveways. Meadows and pastures were also recorded, usually in acres, and the annual value of fisheries was generally shown, often in terms of eels. Mills were recorded by number, and occasionally the annual amount rendered from milling activity. Other information relates to markets, harbours, parks and vineyards. Chart Sutton, Chislet, and Leeds are all recorded as having several arpents of vine, an arpent being a term imported from France, amounting to 100 square perches. Some of these items were recorded for Trimworth Manor as the following record shows.

Domesday and Trimworth Manor

Trimworth was one of 11 manors within the Wye hundred, the others being Beamonston, Eastwell, Boughton Aluph, Buckwell, Wye, Fanscombe, Ashenfield, Combegrove, Brook and Hampton. The entry for Trimworth is as follows:

> ### Land of Hamo the Sheriff in the Lathe of Wye
> *In Wye Hundred*
> *Hamo the Sheriff holds a Manor from the King which answered for two and half sulungs before 1066; now for one sulung and three yokes. Land for eight ploughs. In lordship five ploughing oxen.*

Table 2: Comparison of Domesday settlements in the Stour Valley

Asset given in Domesday	Trimworth	Wye	Godmersham	Chilham
Sulungs	2½	7	8	5
Ploughs	8	52	12	20
Lord's ploughs	5	9	2	2
Villeins	16	114	60	38
Cottars/bordars	15	22	8	12
Ploughs of cottars/bordars	10	17	17	12
Slaves	7	7	2	-
Churches	1	1	1	1
Mills	1	4	1	6½
Meadowland (acres)	20	133	12	9
Woodland pig pastures	30	300	40	80
Value before 1066	£10	£80 10s. 8d.	£12	£40
Value when granted by King William	£7	£125 10s.	£12	£30
Value in 1086	£14 6s. 6d.	£100	£20	£30

Adapted from P. Burnham and M. de Sax, A New History of Wye: The Heritage of a Kent Village, *Wye Historical Society (2003).*

> *Sixteen villagers with fifteen smallholders have ten ploughs.*
> *A church; seven slaves; a mill at nine shillings and sixty eels. Meadow, twenty acres;*
> *woodland, thirty pigs.*
> *Value before 1066 £10; later £7; now £14.6s.6d.*
> *Hugh de Montfort holds three and half yokes of this manor. Value sixty shillings.*

It is interesting to compare the four settlements of Wye, Godmersham, Chilham and Trimworth in the Stour Valley (Table 2). The importance of Wye is shown in the number of ploughs and the very substantial record of meadowland acres and pig pastures, sufficient to support three hundred pigs. Coolings' study of Wye (*A New History of Wye*, see Ch. 6) notes that Wye's pig pastures are one of the largest in Kent. The number of slaves (seven in Trimworth and Wye) is a clear indication that Norman England was a slave-holding society. In both manors, Hugh de Montfort leased land, two yokes in Wye and three and a half yokes in Trimworth. He was one of King William's most senior and powerful Norman barons. Each settlement is recorded as having a church and at least one mill, valued at nine shillings and 60 eels at Trimworth. The comparison below shows Wye to be the dominant community, (Godmersham, however, having more sulungs), and this position has been retained. Godmersham is now a small hamlet and Trimworth a collection of buildings, despite the fact that its importance was indicated in the past by Trimworth being the name of the parish (now Crundale), and for many years Trimworth enjoyed the advowson of the church at Crundale, that is, the legal right to nominate the person to hold church office.

DOMESDAY MONACHORUM

The Church has had a great impact on the landscape and economy of Kent. The foundation of two cathedrals, Canterbury (597) and Rochester (601), together with religious houses and parish churches, underlines the importance of the Church in Kent. Today there are about 430 surviving medieval churches in Kent, and this is barely half the religious buildings that once existed. There were probably 400 Saxon churches in Kent, of which about twenty retain some tangible Saxon remains. Sadly, over 350 will have completely disappeared, although the sites of some are known. The ecclesiastical development of Kent began with the coming of St Augustine and continued without a break for another 600 years, during which 500 parishes were formed dating back to 1100 and beyond. The average parish size is about 2,000 acres but there is a huge variation, ranging from 202 acres in Chillenden to 15,000 in Tonbridge. The evidence for all this ecclesiastical development is unusually rich and abundant in Kent because of the survival of a major early source, the Domesday Monachorum of Christ Church, whose relevance to Trimworth Manor will be illustrated following a description of this major early record.

The Domesday Monachorum is an ancient manuscript, written at the Monastery of Christ Church in Canterbury and preserved in the Library of the Dean and Chapter. It is a beautiful book with the pages adorned by embellishments and coloured capitals. It was written in about 1100 although there appear to be 'three hands' contributing in 1100, 1150 and 1250. The book is in four parts, of which the first is the most relevant to this study.

Part 1 contains documents related to Kentish churches and the payments due to be paid by the parochial clergy, such as chrism fees, paid each Holy Week for the receipt of oil for baptism. It reveals the ecclesiastical structure of Kent, which in turn influenced the arrangements of parishes in medieval England. 'It is clear that churchmen at the end of the eleventh century were familiar with a form of organisation closely akin to the rural deaneries of more recent years.' (Ward, see reference under Sources for Domesday Monachorum). Part 2 surveys the lands of the Archbishop of Canterbury and other Kentish landowners. Part 3 lists knights of the Archbishop. Part 4 contains documents relating to Christ Church Canterbury and its properties.

The Domesday Monachorum and Trimworth Manor

The content most relevant to Trimworth comes in the first section of the manuscript on Kent churches and the payment of dues. In a list headed 'Churches subordinate to Wye' is written:

> *Aescedefford* (Ashford)
> *Crundala* (Crundale)
> *Broca* (Brook)
> *Dreamwurth* (Trimworth)
> *Haenostesyle* (Hinkshill)
> *Brixiestun* (Sevington) (Domesday Book records a church here, and the estate
>   owner was Brixi.)
> *Wyllan* (Eastwell)
> *Haudkashyrste* (Hawkshurst)

In the case of Trimworth, and some others listed here, the church was probably a chapel attached, or located near, to the manor house. Scores of these chapels survive in Kent, but few remain in use and most are in ruins. Many, like Trimworth, have disappeared altogether, although map and documentary evidence supported by geophysical survey have suggested a possible location near to the existing house. Everitt speculates that the origin of these chapels is explained by the scattered nature of settlement in which many farmsteads were remote from the parish church. There are records of manorial lords making the case to the local abbot for a manorial chapel on the grounds of isolation. John Malmaynes, of Stoke at Hoo, argued that being situated at a distance from the parish church often prevented him from attending divine service and requested an oratory for himself and his family. In the Wealden hamlet of Leigh, 'inhabitants were much incommoded by the length and badness of the way to Leigh, and the inundation that frequently happened' (Everitt). In this case and in the case of Trimworth they were not much more than a mile from the church, but on winter days this was a formidable distance on foot. As the population of these rural communities rose, the manorial chapel may have provided a service to the community wider than the manorial household alone. In fact, some became upgraded with their own burial grounds and baptismal rites, though few became entirely independent of the parish church.

The settlement pattern is not the only reason for the growth of these manorial chapels. A further factor would have been the emergence of a manorial gentry, in some cases marrying into Anglo-Saxon families, gaining influence and estates. For such people the right to a chapel was a symbol of pride and success. In the case of Trimworth, these families could have included the de Valoigns and the Hadlows, and later the Kempes and the Filmers.

Returning to the Domesday Monachorum, the second and third parts of the manuscript refer to the names of powerful landlords and their extensive properties in Kent. One of these is Odo of Bayeux, whose wealth and power as Earl of Kent dominated the history of the county following the Conquest. His name occupies a lot of space in both Domesday Book and the Monachorum, such was his influence as the predominant land and property owner, probably being given Trimworth by William. Odo was half-brother of the Conqueror, and his title, Bishop of Bayeux, illustrates his great continental connections. Odo was the cause of many disputes and rebellions. He was accused of unjustly dispossessing the Church and told to make restitution. In 1088, Odo and his vassals were in dispute with the king, who was supported in this instance by Archbishop Lanfranc and other Kentish landowners. Another powerful figure at the time was Hamo (Hamymo, Haimo) the Sheriff, who probably came from western Normandy and was dapifer to William (one who brings meat to the table, the official title of Steward to the King's household.) Hamo died in 1100 and his association with Trimworth is noted in the Domesday Monachorum in the phrase '*Haymo uicommes tenet Dramword pro ii sullinc et dimidio*' (Hamo, viscount, holds Trimworth for two sulungs and a half).

Sources for the Domesday Monachorum

For a translation and interpretation of the content of the Domesday Monachorum, see D.C. Douglas, *Domesday Monachorum*, Royal History Society (1944), available at Canterbury Cathedral Archives and at the Centre for Kentish Studies.

For references to churches listed, see G. Ward, 'The List of Saxon Churches in the Domesday Monachorum and the White Book of St Augustine', *Archeologia Cantiana*, vol. 45 (1933), pp.60 to 89. This article also explains the hierarchy of the churches in Kent.

For an excellent review of the ecclesiastical development of Kent, see A. Everitt, *Continuity and Colonisation: the evolution of Kentish Settlement*, Leicester University Press. This book contains a series of maps to show the geographical development of churches in mid-Kent.

Finally, the Domesday Book classic by H.C. Darby, *The Domesday Geography of South East England*, Cambridge University Press (1962), makes frequent reference to the Domesday Monachorum; see Chapter 10 on Kent.

CHAPTER 6

Early House Occupancy

This chapter is concerned with sources for genealogy, which allow the researcher to gain an insight into the people who resided in a property. It takes us beyond a consideration of bricks and mortar to consider life-stories of people who owned the property, and who had an influence on the surrounding community and its evolving economy. It is a source which personalises our research and adds interest to the process of tracing the history of a house. One of the earliest sources of genealogy is the **Inquisition Post-Mortem** (IPM) which is particularly relevant for larger, older houses, or houses which formed part of an estate. The records survive from around 1240 until the Restoration in 1660, when feudal tenure was abolished.

Before considering the use of the IPM in relation to Trimworth Manor, it may be helpful to describe the landholding under the feudal system, which was established in England and parts of Wales following the Norman Conquest. Basically, the king held all the land, but granted some land to his followers and supporters. They were the 'tenants in chief' and they in turn granted land to their supporters to create a pyramidal structure of landholding. The main unit of land was the 'manor', whose lands often spread out between the lands of nearby manors, each one forming an important social and economic unit. On the death of a feudal 'tenant in chief' (the direct tenant of the Crown), inquiries (the Inquisition) were undertaken to establish what lands were held and who should succeed to them. A local 'escheator' would be responsible for taking possession of the dead tenant's estate, who would then convene a local jury and conduct the inquiry. The earliest Inquisitions record the date of death, the names of manors held, and the services performed in return for them, and also the name, age, and relationship of the heir(s). If the jury noted that the heir was under age (or insane), the lands defaulted to the Crown and were administered on the heir's behalf until he or she became of age (21). The IPM applies generally to the death of 'tenants in chief', but sub-tenants of higher status are often mentioned, and further records are also made of the assignment of the dower (part of the husband's estate to be held by his widow for her lifetime).

THE INQUISITION POST MORTEM RECORDS FOR TRIMWORTH MANOR

Before the IPM records began in the early 13th century, there is documentary evidence that Trimworth was given by William the Conqueror to Bishop Odo of

Bayeux, whose wealth and power as Earl of Kent dominated the history of the county following the Conquest. He was half-brother to the Conqueror and was at the centre of many disputes, including accusations of dispossessing the church (as detailed in Chapter 5, in the section on the Domesday Monachorum). Following his fall from grace, Trimworth came into the hands of Ruallon de Valoigns at the end of King Stephen's reign. This is confirmed in the **Cartulary of Leeds Priory**, which refers to a grant by Reulandus de Waluine of the church of Crundale, otherwise known as *Dromewrda* (note the close form of this name to the Anglo-Saxon *dreaman wyrthe*, the first recorded name for Trimworth). The Cartulary of Leeds Priory is a 12th-century book which records grants and tithes, including reference to Trimworth. An abstract of the book's contents are contained in L. Sherwood's article in *Archaeologia Cantiana* (1951), vol. 64, p.24.

During the reign of Henry II (1154-89), the house remained with the Valoignes, firstly with Alan, and then with Hamo. Later, in the reign of King Henry III, the following reference appears in the Register of the Hospital of St Lawrence, Canterbury: 'Hamonis de Valoins gives to God and the infirm brothers of the Hospital of St Lawrence for the health of his soul, and that of Agnes his wife, the land which Godley de Rall held in the time of Ruoland, the grantor's father.' (Dated at Trimworth, Wednesday after the feast of the Holy Trinity. The year is not given, but is likely to be early in the 13th century, in the reign of Henry III.) Incidentally, the Hospital of St Lawrence was founded in 1137 by Hugh de Trottesclive, outside the walls of Canterbury, primarily as a sanatorium to which monks suffering from contagious diseases such as leprosy might be cared for. Secondly, it acted as an almshouse for relatives of the monks who had fallen into dire poverty (see the Revd C. Woodruff, 'The Register and Chartulary of Saint Lawrence, Canterbury', in *Archaeologia Cantiana* (1939), vol. L, p.33). Hamo was clearly concerned about the safety of his soul, because as well as the gift noted above, he also intended to give the rectory of Crundale to the Priory and Convent of Leeds 'in perpetual arms'. This gift never took place, because his heirs refused to ratify the gift. Instead Archbishop Hubert agreed that Hamo should grant a rent of 25 shillings from his church in 'Dromwoed' to the prior and cannons forever. This reference is found in the **Calendar of Charter Rolls**.

In the first volume of the IPM, covering the period 1216-25, there is a brief reference to the manors of Trimworth and Dodindale, in which the rent is recorded as half a mark and one-and-a-half knight's fee. The mark is not a coin, but is equivalent to the monetary sum of 13s. 4d., half a mark being 6s. 8d. A knight's fee is a feudal term to describe the value of land, and was the amount of money, or service, an estate was required to pay to support one knight, typically around £20 per year *c.*1200. A later reference in 1263 notes that 'they say he had a view from the ville of Hardes, four shillings; Nonnington two shillings; from Blean, 4 shillings; from Tremworth, half a mark; from Sheldwich, 2 shillings'. The term 'view' is the 'view of frank pledge', meaning the right of the domain or estate to hold court-leet, granted by charter to the lord of the manor. The court-leet dealt with local petty offences, maintenance of highways and ditches, and appointed local officers.

At this time, Trimworth became associated with the Haudlo (Hadloe) family, initially John de Handolue, who died in 1283, and then his son John, having 'free warren in all of their demesne lands in Tremworth, Vanne, Eschendene and Ore-by-Middleton in the County of Kent'.

Richard de Hadloe then inherited the estate in 1334. He was described as a Knight, (Chevalier), Earl of Gloucester. The IPM gives details of the land use and rents for Trimworth Manor in 1326 and 1343, which are produced in full in Tables 3 and 4. The estate at this time appeared to be flourishing, with over 300 acres, mainly arable; a watermill, probably located just below the present house on a leat run off the River Stour; and a church. The 1343 entry notes that the manor also continued to hold the advowson of the church at Crundale. The term 'advowson' is important, because it bestowed the legal right of the lord of the manor to nominate a person to hold church office. This was an extraordinary privilege, often exercised without the need to present the nominee to the bishop.

Table 3: Land use, Trimworth, 1326.

Extent or Survey of Tremworth Manor, 1326

Taken at Wy Thursday after Epiphany 20 Ewd. II by Masters John de Podeswell and Tho de Fev'esham.

Jurors: Thomas de Coumbe: Thomas Marischal: Roger de Mershton: John Crulling: Josse atte Stoure: Tho Colebrand: Rich le Hunte: John le Millere: Symon Colebrand: Wm. Scochm: Wm. Elston: John Croysere.

Capital messuage with pasture and produce from garden	2s. per annum
200 acres of arable at 6d. per acre worth	100s. per annum
14 acres of meadow at 3d. per acre	42s. per annum
62 acres pasture at 3d. per acre	15s. 6d. per annum
32 acres woodland	20s. per annum
A water mill	40s. per annum
Rents of assize	£14 14s. 11¾d. per annum
Ploughing service	9s. 8d. per annum
Rents of 43 Tens worth	5s. 4d. per annum
4 score and 10 eggs as payments	7½d. per annum

Of the same land David de Strabolgy holds in his manor of Egarlone from this manor of Tremworth 45 acres of land by service of ¼ of a knight's fee worth 10s. p.a.

Thomas de Coumbe holds from this manor 38 acres in Crundale by service of (½?) part of a knight's fee worth 12s. 8d. p.a.

Thomas Chirche of Canterbury holds 2 carucates of land near Canterbury by mesne tenant service of 1 knights fee worth 5 marks, lately £10, which he pays in rents of assize.

A church worth 17 marks p.a.

Perquisites worth 2s. p.a.

Source: Inquisition Post Mortem.

Table 4: Land use, Trimworth, 1343

Tremworth

1 fee in Holford held of Earl of Gloucester by rent of 2s. 1d. paid at Feast of St Michael
Advowson of Church of Crundale

Capital messuage
250 acres of arable worth £4 3s. 8d.
4 score acres pasture worth 20s. (i.e. 3d. p. acre)
40 acres of 'bosci amput'[a] cut in 8 years 4s.
                         et ore quo anno[b] 20s.
16 acres of meadow worth 32s. per annum (2s. p. acre)
Water mill worth 53s. 4d. per annum
£20 in rents of assize from tenants
Fanne   25½ acres of land value 8s. 6d. p. annum (4d. p. acre)
             50 acres pasture value 12s. 6d. p. annum
             24½ acres of wood (bosci amput) worth 12s. p. annum

Jurors: John de Hadres: William de Trendle: Roger Wiboun: Henry atte Mead: Roger de
Stovolde: Nicholas Elfelm: Robert del Isle: Andr de (?Wodhell): John _____?: William de
_____?: ? Wodenantone
[a] coppice
[b] and worth in that year

Source: Inquisition Post Mortem

When Richard de Hadloe died, the manor passed to his wife Isabelle and on her death in 1361 the heirs were her two daughters, Margaret (26) and Elizabeth (22). Margaret married John de Apelby and Elizabeth married Edmund de la Pole, who was later killed at Agincourt. The value of the manor in 1367 was one knight's fee and a payment of eight shillings to the Abbot of St Augustine's Canterbury, and 11s. 6d. to the Abbott of Battle. The extent of the estate had now fallen to 100 acres, possibly due to the ravages of the Black Death and a consequent shortage of labour. Falling levels of population at such times have clearly been reflected in the extent of land abandonment to scrubland and woodland. The IPM notes that the land at Trimworth 'could be improved by tillage and manuring to the value of sixpence per acre, being worth now four pence per acre as pasture. Forty acres are worth only tuppence per acre because they cannot be sold unless well tilled and manured.'

In 1370, Ingelram de Couci was granted the manor. His tenure was quickly followed by scandal and disgrace. He had married King Edward III's daughter, Isabella, and both became the centre of a controversy resulting in the forfeiture of the manor to the King. The IPM notes that:

> the escheator took into the King's hands the Manors of Tremworthe and Vanne and ten pounds rent in the suburb of Canterbury, which had belonged to Ingleram de Coucy and Isabel his wife and were forfeited to the King because the said Ingram, by his letters patent sealed with his seal and read in Parliament,

surrendered what he held of the King in fee and homage, asserting that he was bound to adhere to the king's adversary in France before all others as his natural and superior Lord. The value of the Manor of Trimworthe together with the rents is 21 pounds two shillings and nine pence.

In November 1377, the Calendar of Patent Rolls records a grant in favour of Isabel(la), daughter of Edward III and aunt of Richard II (who was on the throne at the time), which reads as follows:

> In consideration of her noble birth and for her honourable maintenance whilst in England, the King with the assent of Parliament grants to Alexander, Archbishop of York … all the manors and tenements of … with the exception of the manors of Tremworth and Vanne (co Kent) with the condition that she stays in England, the profits there from shall be kept for her use and paid to her … If, during the said war she voluntarily or otherwise by her husbands command pass beyond the realm … the premises are reseized into the Kings hands.

Her compliance with this command is in doubt, because in 1380 the manor was granted to John Beverlie, who had been Constable of the Castle of Leeds and its fulling mills. At his death in 1381, the manors passed to John Apelby, the King's Esquire, and the Patent Rolls give a full and fascinating account of the condition of the estate and the manor contained in the Inquisition held at Wye in 1380.

> The Manor of Thremworth contains diverse ruinous buildings of no net value, which cannot be repaired or maintained from year to year without help from the issues from the Manor. There are 68 acres of arable worth 22 shillings and 8 pence yearly, 12 acres of meadow worth 36 shillings and 70 acres of pasture worth 11 shillings and 8 pence. 21 acres of wood are of no value because they are all felled when the Manor was in the hands of Ingram Lord of Coucy, and they cannot be felled or turned to profit within ten years of that time. There are 13 pounds 18 shillings of rents of assize; whereof 10 pounds arise from tenements late of John Chicche in the suburbs of Canterbury. There are yearly rents of 24 hens worth 4 shillings, 120 eggs worth six pence and seven plough shares worth 7 shillings. Of these issues the Earl of Stafford receives two shillings and one penny yearly, at his Castle at Tonebrigge as for his honour of Gloucester; and John Parker of Yepeswych, squire of the lady Isabelle, the King's aunt, receives 10 pounds yearly for life for the King's grant. Total net yearly value, seven pounds 18 shillings and 9 pence.
>
> (Calendar of Patent Rolls, 1377-81, p.267).

A year later, on the 20 January 1381, there is further detail on the deterioration of Trimworth Manor.

> A hall and chambers cannot be repaired for less than 20 shillings, a kitchen ruinous to as to the walls and the roof at one end, for not less than 8 pounds and a sheepcote for 20 shillings. These defects arose during the tenancy of the said Ingram. The fencing around the manor needs repair up to 20 shillings but

the default of John Beverlie, late farmer and tenant. A building used as ox stalls cannot be repaired unless rebuilt on account of its age, which will cost not less than 21 (and half) marks besides the old timber which is worth 20 shillings.

(Calendar of Patent Rolls, 1377-81, p.614)

It seems that neglect, principally at the hands of Ingram de Courcy, had brought the manor and estate to a desperate state of decay and dereliction. It was appropriate then that the new 'tenant in chief' should be 'disposer of the kings works pertaining to the art of masonry in the Palace of Westminster and the Tower of London'. This man was Henry de Yevele, the King's Master Mason, who was granted the manors of Trimworth and Vanne in 1389 by Richard II. The grant came with a winter robe at Christmas each year from the Great Wardrobe of the Suit of Esquires plus 25 shillings a year, under the instructions of King Richard, and was paid 'in the hanaper' (i.e., from the Treasury, the origin of the word 'hamper'). Henry was a nationally respected figure whose association with Geoffrey Chaucer and role in the rebuilding of part of Canterbury Cathedral will be reviewed in Chapter 7.

On the death of Henry de Yevele in August 1400 the estate entered a new phase of tenancy which was to last for 150 years. The IPM for 1400 records that Trimworth and Fanscombe, and the advowson of the church in Crundale, should revert to the masters and chaplains of the College of Maidstone. The college was established with a hospital and poor houses by Archbishop Boniface of Canterbury, and under his authority a number of churches and manors reverted to the college. (Further details of the college can be found in the Victoria County History, vol. 2, p.232.)

The day-to-day events of the Trimworth estate during this period are highlighted in an IPM reference to a serious case of venison hunting in 1430, the culprit being John de Pirye, by his own confession. At that time, the neighbouring estate of Olantigh was owned by John Kempe, Archbishop of Canterbury, Chancellor of England and founder of Wye College, so the wrath of the highest authority in the land fell upon poor John Pirye. He was required to reveal the names of others known by him to have been guilty, 'and henceforth he shall not hunt thereupon, nor give aid, counsel or consent to any others so doing'.

Following the suppression of the college in 1549, the manors of Tremworth and Fannes were granted to Sir Thomas Cheyne, Treasurer of the Household and Warden of the Cinque Ports, and thereafter to his son Henry, Lord Cheyne, 'Which manors and other premises … are extended at the clear yearly value of 33 pounds, 12 shillings and a halfpenny, except bells and lead.' The grant came with a yearly rent of £10 out of the manor of Donjeon (Dane John?) in the city of Canterbury, as well as the continued advowson of the rectory of Crundale. The importance of the rectory of Crundale in relation to neighbouring communities at the time is illustrated by the following list taken from the Calendar of Patent Rolls, 12 July 1561 (during the reign of Elizabeth I). The list gives details of yearly rents (equivalent to one tenth of the revenues of the 'benefices'). All are in the Deanery of Bridge.

Table 5: The Filmer Inheritance of Trimworth, 1648-1911

1648	First entry in the Court Manor Rolls: Sir Robert Filmer, in the year that he married Dorothy Tuke. The house had now come into the Filmer family of East Sutton, with whom it remained for over 260 years.
1674	Sir Robert created 1st Baronet.
1675	Sir Robert died; inherited by Sir Robert Filmer, 2nd Baronet, who had married Elizabeth Beversham in 1680.
1720	Sir Robert died, inherited by Sir Edward Filmer, 3rd Baronet, who had 11 sons and nine daughters between 1708 and 1731, but only four sons and three daughters survived him because of smallpox.
1755	Sir Edward died; inherited by Sir John Filmer, 4th Baronet.
1797	Sir John died; inherited by Sir Beversham Filmer, 5th Baronet.
1805	Sir Beversham died; inherited by the Revd Sir Edmund Filmer, 6th Baronet. He married Arabella Honeywood in 1755 (see plaque in Crundale church). She was daughter of Sir John Honeywood, whose first wife was Arabella Goodenough.
1810	The Revd Sir Edmund died and was buried in Crundale. Trimworth inherited by the Revd Sir John Filmer, 7th Baronet, who was born in Crundale.
1834	The Revd Sir John died, inherited by Sir Edmund Filmer, 8th Baronet.
1859	Sir Edmund died, inherited by Sir Edmund Filmer, 9th Baronet, member of Grenadier Guards and MP for West Kent 1859-65.
1886	Sir Edmund died, inherited by Sir Robert Marcus Filmer, 10th Baronet.
1911	Sir Robert Marcus sells Trimworth Manor Farm. He was unmarried and died in 1916.

Chartham	£4	2s.	7d.
Crundale		23s.	1d.
Godmersham		18s.	4½d.
Petham		16s.	1¼d.
Waltham		15s.	6½d.
Chilham		13s.	4d.
Boughton Aluph		11s.	8½d.

Early in the reign of Elizabeth I, the Queen alienated the manor to the Kempe family, with whom it remained for nearly 100 years. Sir Thomas Kempe of Olantigh, the neighbouring manor, inherited Trimworth in 1558, and when he died without male issue in 1607 it passed to his brother Reginald, who was baptised at Eastwell in 1553. (His life as a Jacobean squire is featured as family portrait in Chapter 7.) He married Mary Argall, daughter of Richard Argall of East Sutton, in 1590. On the Jacobean porch at Trimworth Manor today are the coats of arms of the Kempes (three wheat sheaves) and the Argall's (three wheat sheaves and three lions' heads) (Fig. 30). The significance of the inheritance in relation to the house is that the Kempes probably instituted major alterations to the old Wealden hall house by putting in ceilings, raising the roof level of the hall, and adding the fine Jacobean porch.

Reginald Kempe died in 1612 and was buried at Crundale, leaving a son, Thomas, and three daughters. His wife Mary died 10 years later and the inheritance went to the eldest daughter, Ann. Eventually the inheritance was divided, with Trimworth going to another daughter, Amy, who had married Morris Tuke of Essex. Their only daughter, Dorothy, carried the inheritance in 1649 on marriage to Sir Robert Filmer of East Sutton. Trimworth was to grow and prosper under the Filmer family for the next 260 years. The succession of Filmer owners at Trimworth from 1649 to 1911 is shown in Table 5.

THE CHANCERY ROLLS

The IPM is not the only source of medieval genealogy published by the Crown. Many records were maintained by the Chancery, which acted as Royal Secretariat in support of the Exchequer, whose role as we have seen was largely financial. From the end of the 12th century, the Chancery began to record copies of the documents it produced in a series of 'rolls'. The printed versions of these records, mostly indexed by name or estates, are accessible and allow fairly detailed accounts of day-to-day dealings of the manor-holding classes, such as appointments to offices, permission to hold markets, debts, misdemeanours, etc. Other records deal with land inheritance, provision of dower for widows and the wardship of minors. The **Close Rolls** (from 1204) deal with closed letters and convey orders to the officers of the Crown. **Charter Rolls** (1199 to 1517) list the Royal Charters, and the **Fine Rolls** (from 1199) record payments to the Crown and the appointment of escheator and other officials. The **Patent Rolls** began in the early 13th century and consist of grants, liberties and privileges passed by the Lord Chancellor in the name of the sovereign. The preface of the Patent Rolls for 1327-30 notes 'that there is scarcely a subject connected with the history or government of this country or with the most distinguished patronages of the 13th, 14th and 15th centuries which is not illustrated in the Patent Rolls'.

Printed versions of these records are usually available in county libraries and archives and a useful list of these sources is available online at **www.medievalgenealogy. org.uk**. The National Archives also hold many records of these courts, and provide excellent information on their use for title deeds as well as genealogy.

PARISH REGISTERS AND RECORDS

Parish registers are records of baptisms, marriages and burials for a parish. The parish boundary is a largely unchanging administrative unit, and so there is a good chance that the history of a family in a community can be traced back without the concern that boundary changes will have affected the continuity. Records date back to 1538, but few survive before 1600, although you may be lucky. Details are usually fairly minimal, but would possibly allow you to compile a family tree and see how the occupants of your home were related to one another. A search for the parish of

Crundale in the Canterbury Cathedral Archives revealed records of births, marriages and deaths from 1554 to 1808. From that date, it is likely that places of residence will be recorded alongside the individual names, which makes them more valuable to the house historian. Parish records are not stored at the National Archives, but they are likely to be in local or county record offices. If you have problems locating them, two source books will help:

The Phillimore Atlas and Index of Parish Registers, Phillimore (2003).

J. Gipson, *Bishops transcripts and marriage licensed bonds and allegations: a guide to their location and indexes*, Federation of Family History Societies (1997).

You may find that the local record office will also have a catalogue for **parish records**, containing fascinating items other than vital statistics which will have been deposited by previous rectors or churchwardens. A search in the Canterbury Cathedral Archives for the parish of Crundale, for example, revealed examples of the kind of documents, letters and notes that are invariably found in such records.

- 1695. Lease of Crundale Rectory including all the parsonages and glebe lands, houses, barns, stables, outhouses and buildings together with the crops upon the glebe land from Michaelmas 1694 to Michaelmas 1695 (U3/116/3/2).

- 1698 to 1728. A bound Account Book of Mr Forster's Charity. Richard Forster was inducted as rector at Crundale in 1698 and died in 1729 leaving a rectorial library of many valuable items which still exists today as a collection. On his death he left property in the parish to be sold, and the money invested to provide for poor children to be taught to read and repeat the church catechism, and for the relief of poor widows and husbandmen at the rector's discretion. The book is an annual record of recipients. At the back of the book are the names of all the charity children from 1733 to 1768, their dates of admission and discharge and names of parents (U3/116/25/1).

- 1859 to 1949. A bound Filmer Family Charity Account Book. The book lists in detail, year by year, the distribution of money to the aged and poor with the recipients named. The awards were not one-off payments. Widow Harlow received 10s. 6d. in 1860 and was receiving £1 10 years later. Filmer was one of several charities, others being Smith's Charity for widows and invalids, Finch's Charity for the two oldest men, and Philpot's Charity for the mothers of the four largest families.

- 1700. A calculation of the value of woodland and open land for produce. Calculations are projected for the next 100 years.

- 1828. Case and Opinion, concerning trees in Crundale churchyard. This contains a letter to the rector from Edward Knight of Godmersham Park, brother of Jane Austen, saying that he is not aware of any claim on the trees by the church. The opinion from Lincolns Inn was that the churchwardens were entitled to bits that fell from trees, and trees that died, but that they might not replace the trees because the soil on which they grew did not belong to the churchwardens!

- 1840/1. Bill for repair of church, and materials.

July 18th		
Man and labour for 1 day	6s.	0d.
Lime and hair	1s.	0d.
Whitening and size	3s.	0d.
August 8th		
Man for ¼ day		10½d.
3 hods mortar	1s.	6d.
½ bundle single laths, 300 nails	2s.	6d.
December 26th		
Man and boy, ½ day	2s.	3d.
Lime and hair	1s.	0d.
February 6th		
Man and boy for ½ day	1s.	2d.
	19s.	**3½d.**

(U3/116/5/1)

- 1900. Will of the Revd Francis Filmer

I give and bequeath to the Minister and Churchwardens for the time being of the said parish of Crundale the sum of £19 9s. upon trust to divide the same at Christmas next ensuing, amongst the most infirm and aged Parishioners of that Parish, preference being given to those who have been most exemplary for their sober, industrious and virtuous habits and those who being in like manner exemplary, have large families.

John Anstey, Executor
(U3/116/25/4)

These examples reveal fascinating insights of village life which are of value to the house and family historian, especially when combined with other documentary sources.

THE FEET OF FINES

The Feet of Fines was an agreement reached between two parties on a dispute over land law, rent dispute or land ownership. The concord was written in triplicate on a sheet of parchment, with two copies side by side and a third along the foot of the parchment. The three copies were separated by a wavy line. One copy was given to the purchaser, another to the vendor and the third, the foot, was retained by the Court of Common Pleas. The document thus became known as the Feet of Fines, and in the case of a local query or dispute it could be pieced together. The concept began in the 1160s and an early example relating to Trimworth was found in the **Kent Feet of Fines** for 1218/19 conducted at Bermondsey on behalf of Hamo de Valoines, Gervase de Aldemanes and his wife Agnes. The manors in question were Trimworth and Dudingdale (Canterbury), and the dispute concerned inheritance and rents relating to the two manors. The documents, however, are of limited use to the house historian apart from indicating ownership and tenancies of the property and land, together with the outcome of disputes. They are not easy to interpret and until 1733 are likely to be written in Latin. Records for 1182 to 1833 are held in the National Archives.

Conclusion

This chapter has been concerned with sources providing details of parish life and early house occupancy. In the case of Trimworth, the earliest records probably relate to a house which has long since disappeared, but the house name lives on. The importance of the estate has been shown by the fact that the parish took its name from the manor before it became Crundale. Further importance was revealed in the legal right of the lord of the manor to appoint people to hold church office. It has also been possible to trace the changing fortunes of the house and its estate and speculate on the causes of these changes. Treason, disease and war have all been part of the story, bringing the estate at various times to near dereliction and decay. At other times, the Crown has granted the manor to individuals holding a key role in the nation's history, such as Henry Yevele. Powerful landowners such as Kempe and Filmer have worked to produce a flourishing estate with large farms playing a vital role in the evolving economic life of the community.

It is often assumed that the research in house occupancy begins with the census returns of 1801. This chapter has illustrated the value of the use of earlier documents, particularly for larger rural houses or those forming part of an estate.

CHAPTER 7

Shadows of the Past: Three Family Portraits

It is stirring to discover the names of people who used to live in your home, especially when their life story is interesting and unusual, and comes from the distant past. How different was the house then? What did these former residents do for a living? These people regarded your house as a home too, and it is fascinating to confront these shadows of the past. It makes us realise that we are merely the present custodians of a house with a long and colourful history of previous occupants. This chapter briefly investigates the lives of three previous Trimworth occupants: a medieval stonemason, a Jacobean squire, and an 18th-century gentleman farmer.

HENRY YEVELE

> Grant for life, as from Michaelmas last, to Henry Yevele, the late King's Master Mason, of the manors of Trimworth and Vannes, Co. Kent, to the value of £17 a year, lately held by John de Appelby, one of the King's Esquires.
> (Calendar of Patent Rolls, 22 October 1389, Richard II)

This man, so favoured by the King, was the 'disposer of the King's works pertaining to the art of masonry in the Palace of Westminster and the Tower of London'. He became the King's Master Mason and one of the finest architects of the Middle Ages.

Henry was born around 1320 at Yeavely in Derbyshire (hence de Yevele). He probably knew Court French and Latin, and possessed a profound knowledge of geometry, learning drawing and carving from his father. Henry travelled widely, and was strongly influenced by Early Perpendicular work, especially at Litchfield and the magnificent Lady Chapel of the rebuilt cathedral. He also became familiar with military buildings and fortifications, and by 1356, when he was in his mid-30s, he was regarded as one of the chief London masons. He was fortunate to survive the plague which decimated the population of England and devastated London; paradoxically it provided the great chance for Henry and his brother Robert to become established as carvers of tombs and monuments. His growing influence brought a contract to upgrade Edward the Black Prince's home at Kennington, two miles south of London Bridge, for which he was paid £221 4s. 7d. On the strength of this work, the Prince appointed him as his personal mason.

Other work was needed at palaces, castles, and manors throughout the country. The hour had come for Henry and he was caught up in a frenzy of new building authorised by King Edward III, who is recognised as one of the greatest patrons of architecture in English history. Works included domestic and civil buildings as well as military, ecclesiastical and monumental works. He had become a huge success and was on the verge of fame (Table 6).

In 1378, Canterbury obtained a writ from the Crown authorising the deployment of masons to Kent to work on the city walls including the building of the West Gate, for which Henry Yevele was the architect. Further commissions followed, including an altar screen in Durham Cathedral, Selby Abbey, and the church and college of Arundel (for which Henry Yevele was influential in the design if not the actual building). His connections with Canterbury at this time were very close, and this continued over the next 10 years partly because of the anxiety to improve defences along the channel coasts, such as Bodiam Castle. In order for him to undertake this work in the south-east, the King granted to him the manors of Trimworth and Vannes with a cash allowance of 25 shillings a year to make up the difference between the issue of these manors and his old fee of £18 5s. Geoffrey Chaucer had been appointed Clerk of the Works to the King in 1389, and the close association between Chaucer and Yevele was unquestionable, initially because both felt they had been treated badly in financial terms. Their pay had been allowed to fall into arrears, and Chaucer's pension had been discontinued. It was because of this that Henry was granted property, to make his income less dependent on the Exchequer.

The link with Chaucer was inevitably reinforced by the fact that Chaucer was Yevele's paymaster, but also Chaucer must have made frequent visits to Canterbury to see works on the castle, walls and cathedral, staying at Trimworth on his visits. It is not perhaps fanciful to contemplate the two of them travelling to Canterbury together, for it was about this time, 1390, that Chaucer was writing the *Canterbury Tales* and could have obtained local colour by walking the Pilgrim's Way with Yevele between Trimworth and Canterbury. Yevele may even have been one of the first to hear these tales!

Yevele was now about 70 years of age but remained incredibly active, with commissions from Richard II for a castle in Winchester, work on the Tower of London and the castle in Canterbury. So heavy were his civic responsibilities that he was given exemption from serving on juries and inquests. The reconstruction of Westminster Hall was a major undertaking for which Yevele decided to return the old shell of the hall, but reworked it to appear entirely new. 'Yevele's genius for simplicity combined with beautiful composition and massing made the Hall a perfect foil for the rich detail of Herland's lovely roof above.' (J. Harvey, *Henry Yevele, the life of an English Architect*, 1944; this has been a useful source.) Yevele was now a grand old man, yet he was still producing masterpieces of design and construction. In his final years, great works were nearing completion at Westminster Hall, Westminster Abbey nave, and Canterbury Cathedral nave. Henry's work on Canterbury Cathedral can be dated to three major periods. In 1363 he was engaged in transforming part of the crypt into a Chancery Chapel for his patron, the Black Prince. From 1377 to 1381 he worked on the side walls of aisles in the nave and returned to work in the nave in 1391. John Harvey in his critique of Henry's work notes the following:

Table 6: Henry Yevele's works in architecture: a chronological table.

Works certainly ascribed are shown in capitals, if doubtful in lower case; destroyed works are in italics.

Domestic and Civic

1358	KENNINGTON MANOR (*part*)		1376	LONDON: SAVOY PALACE (*part*)
1362	WESTMINSTER: ABBOT'S HOUSE, ETC.		1380	Arundel College
1365	WESTMINSTER: PALACE CLOCK TOWER		1383	ROCHESTER BRIDGE
?	LONDON BRIDGE (*parts*)		1389	LONDON: TOWER WHARF
1370	Cobham College, Kent		1395	WESTMINSTER HALL
1372	CHELMSFORD: MOULSHAM BRIDGE			

Military

1361	*Queenborough Castle*		1383	Saltwood Castle
	LONDON: TOWER; BLOODY TOWER, ETC.	1385		CANTERBURY: CITY WALLS
1378	CANTERBURY: WEST GATE			Bodium Castle (parts)
1380	*THAMES DEFENCE TOWERS*		1390	WINCHESTER CASTLE (repairs)
	COWLING CASTLE			CANTERBURY CASTLE (repairs)
	Arundel Castle: Great Hall, etc			

Ecclesiastical

1351	*London: St Katherine's-by-the-Tower*		1379	*BATTERSEA CHURCH:*
1352	Westminster Abbey: South Cloister			*EAST WINDOW*
1380	Arundel Collegiate Church		1381	*LONDON: ST DUNSTAN IN*
1362	WESTMINSTER ABBEY:			*THE EAST (South aisle and porch)*
	NAVE AND WEST CLOISTER		1384	London Bridge: St Thomas's Chapel
1363	Canterbury Cathedral: Black Prince's Chantry		1391	CANTERBURY CATHEDRAL:
1370	Cobham Church, Kent: tower, etc.			NAVE (2nd Work)
1371	LONDON CHARTERHOUSE		?	Meopham Church (New Work)
1377	CANTERBURY CATHEDRAL:		1395	Maidstone Church and College
	NAVE (First Work)			

Monumental

1360	*London: St Paul's:*		1379	Durham Cathedral: Neville Screen
	Tomb of Sir John Beauchamp		?	Selby Abbey: Sedilia
1370	Cobham Church, Kent: Sedilia, etc.		1380	Arundel Church: Pulpit
1372	London: Charterhouse;		1389	WESTMINSTER ABBEY:
	Tomb of Sir Walter Manny			TOMB OF CARDINAL LANGHAM
1373	Lewes Priory (now Chichester Cathedral):			*London: St Paul's; Tomb of Simon Burley*
	Tombs of Earl and Countess of Arundel		1395	WESTMINSTER ABBEY:
1374	*LONDON: ST PAUL'S;*			TOMB OF RICHARD II AND ANNE
	TOMB OF JOHN OF GAUNT		?	London: St Bartholomew the Great; 1376
	Canterbury Cathedral: Tomb of Black Prince			Tomb of Rahere
1377	LONDON: ST PAULS'S;			
	TOMB OF EDWARD III			

(*From J. Harvey,* Henry Yevele, the Life of an English Architect, *1944*)

In many details and as a whole, the nave of Canterbury Cathedral is the very finest product of English gothic. The magnificent compound piers give assurance of stability, and the triple shafts, which carry the high vault, lead the eye upwards to lierne tracery above. The vaulting itself is more perfectly proportioned and poised than any other extant example. The ribs grow with lovely sweeping curves from the shafts … Altogether, the nave of Canterbury Cathedral is the finest interior now remaining in England, and one of the great masterpieces of the world.

John Harvey from whose work this passage was taken also wrote about Yevele in *Archeologia Cantiana,* vol. 56 (1943) and vol. 57 (1944). Most recently, in 1985, he published an article in the *Canterbury Cathedral Chronicle,* vol. 79 (pp.20-32), in which he presents a robust and very convincing argument refuting the claim that Thomas of Hoo was the architect of the nave, and not Henry Yevele. The article contains fascinating insights on building costs, craftsmen, etc.

It must have given Yevele great satisfaction to visit these huge monuments to his designs. He was probably wealthy, with income from his manors in Kent and other properties, besides his professional engagements. He lived the life of a country gentleman, a deeply religious man. In 1400 he made his will and died on 21 August. Chaucer followed him a few weeks later. On the death of Henry the manor reverted to the King and was then granted for life to Henry Longdon. It was worth £20 pounds per year, 'with all profits and commodities'.

Portraits of Henry Yevele

Portrait heads of craftsmen, carved in wood or stone, are quite common in medieval building, and it is possible that three exist for Henry Yevele. Harvey is 'practically certain that one of the label-stops of the arch leading from Westminster Cloister to the courtyard of the Abbots House (Deanery) was intended as his portrait'. This portrait is decayed and the features are severely eroded. The new choir of the Hospital of St Catherine-by-the-Tower, built by Queen Philippa from 1351 to her death in 1369, is now gone, but the choir stalls dating from 1365 remain. Among the misericord carvings is the head of a man wearing the round cap usually associated with the Master of the Works. It is a strong face with a wrinkled forehead, firm nose, prominent cheek-bones, long, thick curling hair, forked beard and curling moustaches. From the detail of the stalls, Harvey asserts there can be little doubt that they were made by royal craftsmen, of whom Yevele had been chief since 1360.

Thirdly, there is a boss in the east walk of the cloisters, just outside the Chapter House door at Canterbury Cathedral. It is a face of an old man whose features are strikingly similar to the St Catherine's head. The eyes are

42 Boss of Henry Yevele, Canterbury Cathedral Cloisters
The boss is located outside the Chapter House door in the cloisters and is considered to be the great architect of the Middle Ages, resident at Trimworth from 1389 until his death in 1400.

closed, indicating that the subject was dead when the boss was carved. Is this Henry Yevele, one of the greatest architects of the Middle Ages, and resident of Trimworth Manor, who died in 1400? (Fig. 42).

REGINALD KEMPE, A JACOBEAN SQUIRE

At the end of the 13th century, Olantigh House, the neighbouring property to Trimworth, came into the hands of the Kempe family through Ralph Kempe, a tenant of Battle Abbey, and known to be living in Wye in 1283. One hundred years later, in 1380, a son was born to Thomas Kempe, a gentleman of Olantigh in the parish of Wye. The son was John Kempe, educated at Merton College, Oxford, who became an English Cardinal, Archbishop of Canterbury and Chancellor of England. He practised initially as an ecclesiastical lawyer before passing into royal service as Chancellor of the Duchy of Normandy. In 1419 he became Bishop of Rochester, and gradually became less involved in politics, being appointed a cardinal in 1439 and Archbishop of Canterbury in 1452. As Richard of York gained influence, Kempe became unpopular, attracting the title 'the Cursed Cardinal'. He died suddenly in 1454, and was buried in the choir at Canterbury Cathedral. Despite his critics, many of whom accused him of neglecting his dioceses, he was an active politician and faithful servant of Henry VI, who regarded him as 'one of the wisest lords of the land'.

There followed a succession of Kempes with various titles and royal roles until, with the death of Sir Thomas Kempe in 1607 (buried at Wye), Trimworth came into the hands of his brother Reginald, there being no son to carry the inheritance. Not a great deal is known about this Trimworth resident. He was baptised at Eastwell, a few miles from Wye, in 1553. When he was about seven, he had a legacy from his grandfather, Sir Thomas Moyle of Eastwell, in the form of a share of his town house in Newgate Street London. Under the same will, his elder brother did rather better, inheriting lands at Dartford, Sutton-at-Hone and Chartham, although this probably came to Reginald on the death of his brother in 1607. Reginald married Mary, the daughter of Richard Argall of East Sutton near Maidstone, in 1590. In the marriage licence, dated 11 December, he is described as 'a gent of Wye', and she as 'of Sutton, virgin'. On their arrival at Trimworth, it is likely that they began to make substantial changes to the old Wealden hall house. They certainly built the elegant Jacobean porch which bears their coats of arms (Fig. 30).

They probably also began extending the house by putting additional floors into the one-storey hall house, to accommodate a growing family. By his wife Mary, Reginald had the following children:

- Thomas, who was to inherit Olantigh.

- John, baptised at Wye in 1594, who had the reversion to Olantigh under certain limitations.

- Ann, baptised at Wye in 1595, who married Josiah Clarke to whom she conveyed the manor of Stowting in 1622.

- Amy, baptised at Wye in 1598 and who married Morris Tuke Esquire, of Layer Marney, Essex, whose family held that manor.

Of great importance to the history of Trimworth was that the last child, Amy, had a daughter called Dorothy who was to marry Sir Robert Filmer of East Sutton. The house reverted to Sir Robert and remained with the Filmers for the next 260 years.

Reginald Kempe died in 1611 and was buried at Crundale. His will, dated 2 January 1610, describes him as 'Renold Kempe, of Trimworth, in County Kent Esquire'. He expressed a wish to be buried at Wye, amongst 'the rest of my ancestors'. (Hasted says he was buried at Crundale.) His will requests that his lands be passed to his son Thomas Kempe 'for the continuance of our sheefe [chief] house of Olantye'. However, before 1617, the sons of Reginald Kempe must have died, otherwise the administration of the estate would have passed to the eldest son instead of the daughter, Ann. Both sons Thomas and John had died without issue.

As we have seen, Reginald Kempe's notable contribution to the house at Trimworth is the fine Jacobean porch. The Jacobean era coincided with the reign of James I (1603-25). Jacobus was the Latin form of James, and the period is associated with a style of architecture, arts and literature. In the year Reginald Kempe came to Trimworth, the first British colony on the North American continent was being founded at Jamestown. Two years previously, the gun powder plot was exposed and the convicted English Catholics, headed by Guy Fawkes, were hanged, drawn and quartered. The residents of Trimworth at that time were probably more concerned about continued outbreaks of the bubonic plague, as well as a severe economic depression which was a feature of the Jacobean period. How familiar were they with the great advances in the areas of navigation, cartography, and surveying being made at the time? Did the walls of Trimworth resound to the recitals of new plays written by Shakespeare? Were the customs of the house affected by the sweeping change of tobacco use? (Despite James' I condemnation of tobacco in 1604, the Virginian colony prospered on this growing English habit, which led to 7,000 tobacconists and smoking houses in London in 1602!).

Further details of the Kempe family can be found in *A General History of the Kemp and Kempe Families*, Leadenhall Press (1902). Especially relevant is Chapter 7 on the Kempes of Wye. This publication is available at the Centre for Kentish Studies.

Sir Edward Filmer,
an 18th-century Gentleman Farmer

The Filmers are a prominent Kent family who owned East Sutton Place near Maidstone from the early 17th century (Table 7). Sir Robert Filmer was born in 1586 at East Sutton, studied at Trinity College, Cambridge, and became an ardent supporter of the King's cause, for which Charles gave him a knighthood. Robert was imprisoned in Leeds Castle and, according to Hasted, his house at East Sutton was plundered by Parliamentary troops on 10 separate occasions. He became famous for his publication *Patriarcha, or the Natural Power of Kings*, published in 1680, 20 years after his death. Robert's eldest son, Edward, took up support for the King while his father was under restraint. He eventually died, unmarried, in Paris in 1669, and his body was brought to East Sutton. The next son, Robert, became a barrister at Gray's Inn, and in May 1648 married Dorothy Tuke, the only daughter of Maurice and Amy Tuke, whose father, as we have seen, was Reginald Kempe. By this marriage, the Filmer family became associated with Trimworth Manor and the advowson of the church of Crundale. Robert was also staunchly royalist and faced difficult times, dying in 1675 and being buried at East Sutton. There were four other sons, three dying in infancy, and the fourth, Samuel, emigrated to Virginia, following his uncle Sir Henry Filmer who had established plantations there. (See *From Kent to Virginia, historic links between county and state*, Kent Archives.) Moving down the Filmer family descendents we come to the subject of our study, Sir Edward Filmer, the 3rd Baronet, whose son was born at East Sutton in 1683, educated at New College, Oxford and who then became directly involved in the management of the family estates, including Trimworth. Sir Edward had a remarkable number of 20 children, but of the 11 sons, five died of smallpox. Of the remaining sons, two came of age, married, then died without heirs. The others never married, so despite the large number of children, only one, Edmund, produced heirs. (He was the 6th Baronet and he married Annabella Christina Honeywood. While searching through these family trees, it was a great surprise for the author to see that Annabella's mother's maiden name was Goodenough!)

Incidentally, Sir Edmund carried the family tradition of being associated with law, army or the Church. He was the Reverend Sir Edmund Filmer, rector of Crundale church, and there is a wonderful inscription in the church to his wife Annabella. 'She was the most dutiful and affectionate wife, a kind and tender parent, and indulgent mistress, and as a Christian, true exemplary for her piety, charity and humility.' She died in October 1798, aged 70, and was survived by seven of her nine children, eight of whom had been born in Crundale.

But back to our subject, Sir Edward Filmer. The extent of his estates was impressive, consisting of East Sutton Place with its farmland, 400 acres of woodland and estates in Kingsnorth (Ulcomb), Hoathly in Lamberhurst, Wichling, Hinkshill in Wye, Godmersham and Trimworth in Crundale. In 1740, it was valued at £1,620, and most of it was leased to tenants. It is likely that his holdings were similar in size and extent to many other landowners in Kent at the time. Sir Edward had inherited the estates in 1720, when his father, Sir Robert Filmer, died. (Chapter 9 refers to an estate map of Trimworth, which was drawn up in 1720 at the time of this change of inheritance.) Well before his father's death, Sir Edward had taken a keen interest in the running of the estate. Agricultural methods and techniques were a major pre-occupation for him, as illustrated in the copious and detailed records he kept. Crop rotation was keenly practised, and he developed a flexible rotation of turnips; barley and clover seed after a summer fallow; wheat upon the clover lay; peas, beans or tares; oats; summer fallow. This was an extended version of the Norfolk rotation

Table 7: The Filmer Family Tree

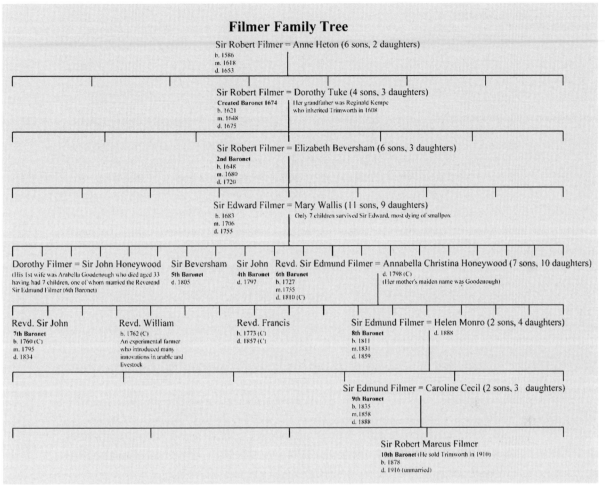

of turnips, barley, clover, wheat. The farming notes contain some useful reminders; 'February, May, June, dig hop gardens, but don't let boys dig them in' and 'Buck wheat, one bushel sows an acre which ploughed in mid-summer will mend it as good as twenty loads of dung an acre.'

The farm accounts note the value of crops produced on the farm, most of them being sold, but in the early 1720s he estimated that 20 seams (i.e., 160 bushels) of wheat and 30 seams of barley were needed for household use. Arable was much more important than pasture. Labour payments were recorded for sowing, digging, weeding, hoeing, mowing, reaping, charcoal burning, clay burning, mole catching, all paid by piece work. Produced below is a typical day labourer's contract (Table 8).

Marling was another activity, particularly important on the lighter soils of the Weald, where a mixture of clay and lime improved the soil structure. It was a practice in use in medieval times, and proved popular again in the 17th century, as

Table 8: A day labourer's contract, 1728.

> **5 February 1727-8**
>
> Bargain'd with Edward Mercer for a day labourer at 1s. 4d. per diem from Ladyday to Michaelmas, at 1s. 2d. per diem from Michaelmas to Ladyday. The days he hunts the hares 1s. per diem, his meat and drink as Sir Edward Filmer's other menial servants have, but when he works as a day labourer to be us'd only as they are who work for the said Sir Edward Filmer.
>
> The said Edward Mercer has hired of the said Sir Edward Filmer a house and plot called the Parish House and to keep a hog, at the rate of 40s. per annum half yearly be paid.
>
> This contract is to subsist from year to year, till notice is given, six months notice shall be given either side before 2 witnesses the day after and not upon the day, that any dispute shall or may hapen to arise between the contracting partys, and 'tis further between the said partys that when the said Edward Mercer shall be requir'd to mow the bowling green or grass walks of the [missing] Sir Edward Filmer in the summer time before the usual hour that days works begin, he the said Edward Mercer shall have liberty that morning to have his breakfast with the said Sir Edward Filmer's servants, in consideration thereof.

From Kentish Sources III: Aspects of Agriculture and Industry, *ed. E. Melling, K.C.C. (1961), p.54.*

illustrated in Gervase Markham's *Enrichment of the Weald of Kent*, which advocated 500 cartloads per acre. Imagine the labour requirement! Pay was one shilling for every ten marl cartloads, and half a crown for every new hole dug before the marl was reached, which could have been up to six feet. Often the pits filled with water and men had to 'set up all night to draw the water'. These documents provide fascinating insights into the farming year in the early part of the 18th century and indicate the strong personal involvement of Sir Edward in the practice and management of farms and farming. It was an activity taken up by later Filmer descendants. Sir Edward's grandson, the Revd Sir William Filmer, was born at Crundale in 1762. He was a Bachelor of Divinity and an experimental farmer. Arthur Young commented on many of his inventions and improved techniques, such as a six-course crop rotation, greater use of swedes, sanfoin and lentils, and the breeding of Leicester sheep and Berkshire pigs. The Revd Sir William died unmarried in 1830.

The Filmer story at Trimworth ends with the 10th Baronet, Sir Robert Marcus Filmer, born in 1878 and remaining unmarried. He had three sisters and a brother, who died aged one, thus bringing this branch of the Filmer line to an end. Sir Marcus sold Trimworth in 1910 and the extent of the estate is shown in detailed land sale documents described in Chapter 10. So ended a 260-year association between Trimworth and the Filmers, which began in 1648 with Sir Robert Filmer and ended with the death of Sir Robert Marcus Filmer in 1910 (Table 8). Further details on the Filmer family, which have been used in the compilation of this section, can be found in the three volumes written by Bruce John Filmer, *Filmer Family Note*, available at the Centre for Kentish Studies.

Details of the sources referred to on farming can be seen in *Aspects of Agriculture and Industry*, edited by Elizabeth Melling and published by Kent County Council in 1961, under the general series of Kentish Sources.

CHAPTER 8

Later House Occupancy

From the early 19th century, both the house historian and the genealogist have the benefit of a comprehensive, well-organised and accessible resource which will take their research into the lives of people who have resided in their house. It is a resource which presents an important opportunity to personalise your research beyond the physical structure of the property, allowing you to understand the community in which the house is located, as well as identifying major life-events affecting the household. This resource is the census return, compiled to help the government of the day to gather information about population size, structure and change. It has allowed the government to identify spatial change in the size and distribution of regional and local populations, helping them to plan for service provision and employment. Census information is 'closed' for a period of 100 years to protect the confidentiality of personal details. Thus the 1901 returns were not released until 2002 and are the latest currently available.

CENSUS RETURNS FOR THE UK

With the exception of 1941, a census of population has been taken every 10 years since 1801, when the government wanted to know how many men were available to resist Napoleon, should he invade our shores. The information collected up to 1831 was therefore very basic, consisting of questions on the number of houses and families, number of people, the number involved in agriculture, trade, manufacturing and other occupations, and also some information on baptisms, burials and marriages. From 1841 the census returns were compiled using the same system of registration districts and sub-districts that were used for the registration of births and deaths, so there is a direct link between these most important 19th-century sources. Each sub-district was further sub-divided into enumeration districts covering a defined area of the city or county. It was the responsibility of the enumerator to ensure that people living there on the night of the census were included in the returns. Inevitably there was an undercount, which would have been greatest in the poorer parts of the country, or where population was most dense, with many people having 'no fixed abode'. Returning to the content of the 1841 census, the following information was collected for individuals:

1. forenames and surnames,
2. ages

3. sex,
4. occupations,
5. information on place of birth, including 'foreign parts'.

From 1851 to 1891, the information was expanded to include:

1. full name,
2. age,
3. marital status,
4. relationship to head of household,
5. gender,
6. occupation,
7. parish and county of birth,
8. whether blind, deaf or dumb.

Even fuller information comes with the 1901 returns such as: road, name or number of house, whether inhabited or uninhabited, and the number of rooms (if less than five). This last measure was meant to be an indicator of poverty.

These returns allow the house historian to work backwards decade by decade, building up a picture of change or continuity, as will be seen in relation to Trimworth later in this section. However, the researcher should be aware of certain limitations. The return was made for one given day of the year, and if the house was not occupied on that day, it will not appear in the records. Secondly, earlier returns do not always include street names or numbers and also house numbers and names can change over time. Thirdly, the house occupier may not be the house owner. This has been the case for Trimworth for generations, and therefore other sources are required to find out about the property owner and the important role he has played in the transfer of this particular property. With these reservations in mind, the census returns remain one of the most rewarding and accessible sources for tracing the history of your house.

Census Returns and the House Historian: The Example of Trimworth Manor

In Ireland's *History of the County of Kent*, written in 1829, reference is made to the 1821 census in which the parish of Crundale is recorded as having 250 inhabitants, of which 123 were male and 127 female. Over the next 100 years the population of Crundale fluctuated as the figures below demonstrate (Table 9).

The period 1851 to 1861 is one of modest population growth for Crundale, perhaps in the response to the need for more agricultural and domestic labour in rural areas now required to feed growing urban and industrial populations. However, the period 1891 to 1901 records a substantial population decline, particularly female. This may be the response to better employment opportunities in urban areas. In 1851, half of the country's population resided in cities. By 1901 this figure had risen to three-quarters.

Table 9: Census of population returns for Crundale, 1821-1901

Date	Total Pop	% Change	Male	% Change	Female	% Change	Inhabited Houses	Uninhabited Houses
1821	250		123		127			
1841	278	11	143	16	135	6	42	
1851	227	-18	121	-15	106	-21	47	4
1861	279	23	148	22	131	24	53	1
1871	257	-8	129	-13	128	-2	55	-
1881	275	7	141	9	134	5	60	1
1891	257	-7	127	-10	130	-3	59	5
1901	213	-17	115	-9	98	-25	52	5

Source: Census of Population.

The **1841 census** records the following inhabitants and their ages for Trimworth Farm:

George Parkins	77	farmer
? Allan	30	
Elizabeth Culver	40	
Sarah Pemble	16	
Daniel Pilcher	33	
George Pilcher	30	
Edmund Hoar	19	
Sophie Neale	16	

The household therefore consisted of an elderly farmer, aged 77, with domestic servants and farm labourers, all born within the county.

The **1851 census** gives more detailed information of a household consisting of 12 people, none of whom were present 10 years earlier. Trimworth is described as a farm of 250 acres, employing nine labourers and three boys. The tenant farmer was James Tassel, aged 54, who lived with his 49-year-old wife, Mary, and their three sons and one daughter. There were two young house servants and four farm servants. Places of birth were all local: Brook (four), Thanington, Waltham, Chilham (three), Wye, and the most distant being Canterbury.

By **1861**, the household had fallen in size to five inhabitants. Only James and Mary Tassel and their daughter Elizabeth remained from 1851, but they had been joined by an 84-year-old mother-in-law and a 19-year-old dairy maid born in Molash. The farm had increased slightly to 260 acres and employed seven labourers, four carters, and a boy.

Table 10: Census return for Trimworth, 1891.

Administrative County of Kent — The undermentioned Houses are situate within the Boundaries of the — Page 2

Civil Parish of Crundale; ~~Municipal Borough~~ of; ~~Municipal Ward~~ of; ~~Urban Sanitary~~ District of; ~~Town or Village or Hamlet~~ of; Rural Sanitary District of East Ashford; Parliamentary ~~Borough or~~ Division of Ashford; Ecclesiastical Parish ~~or District~~ of Crundale

Cols. 1: No. of Schedule	2: ROAD, STREET, &c., and No. or NAME of HOUSE	3: HOUSES Inhabited	4: HOUSES Uninhabited (U.) or Building (B.)	5: Number of rooms occupied if less than five	6: NAME and Surname of each Person	7: RELATION to Head of Family	8: CONDITION as to Marriage	9: AGE last Birthday of Males	10: AGE last Birthday of Females	11: PROFESSION or OCCUPATION	12: Employer	13: Employed	14: Neither Employer nor Employed	15: WHERE BORN	16: If (1) Deaf-and-Dumb (2) Blind (3) Lunatic, Imbecile or Idiot
4	Little Olantigh Cottage	1		4	Elizabeth Hibbard	Head	Wid		67	Housekeeper Dom				Kent – Brook	
					Henry Do	Son	S	30		Agricultural Labourer		X		Do Wye	
5	Trimworth Cottages	1			Charles W. Tarby	Head	M	46		Stone Carter	X			Sussex Battle	
					Louisa Do	Wife	M		38					Do Do	
					Edgar W. Do	Son	S	18		Agricultural Labourer		X		Do Ashburnham	
					May L. Do	Daur			10	Scholar				Do Newfield	
					Gertrude M. Do	Do			6	Do				Do Do	
					Charles A. Do	Son		4		Do				Do Battle	
					Frederick G. Do	Son		4m						Kent Crundale	
6	Do	1			John Taylor	Head	M	28		Agricultural Labourer		X		Do Tenterden	
					Fanny Do	Wife	M		24					Do Kingsnorth	
					Louisa Do	Daur			3					Do Do	
					Nellie Do	Do			1					Do Wye	
7	Trimworth Farm	1			James Benton	Head	M	73		Farmer	X			Do Ashford	
					Charlotte G. Do	Wife	M		71					Do Do	
					Louisa Do	Daur	S		36	Farmers Daughter				Do Do	
					James Do	Son	M	42		Do Son		X		Do Do	
					Mary E. Do	Daur in Law	M		23					Do Little Chart	
					Nellie L. Do	Grand Daur			13	Scholar				Do Ashford	
					Annie M. Do	Do			11	Do				Do Willesborough	
					Fred G. Do	Grand Son		9		Do				Do Ashford	
					Mable J. Do	Do Daur			6					Do Do	
					Mildred Do	Do Do			4					Do Crundale	
	Total of Houses and of Tenements with less than Five Rooms	4		1	Total of Males and Females			9	14						

NOTE.—Draw the pen through such of the words of the headings as are inappropriate. Eng.—Sheet A.

Reproduced with permission of the Kent Archives Service and the Centre for Kentish Studies.

By **1871**, a more substantial increase in farm size had taken place. The census recorded a farm of 366 acres, now employing 13 men and six boys. The new tenant was John Henham, from East Peckham, a widower of 37, and his six daughters and one son, with ages of 5, 6, 7, 9, 11, 12, and 13 years. The household, not surprisingly, also contained a governess, born in Lancashire, and two servants, one born in Hampshire and the other described as a 16-year-old housemaid from Godmersham. The census was now requiring information on whether inhabitants were deaf and dumb, blind, imbecile, idiot or lunatic.

By **1881**, the farm had grown by well over fifty per cent to 570 acres, employing 27 men and three boys. However, the residents of Trimworth had fallen to only two local unmarried brothers, Austin and Valentine Gambrill, aged 40 and 27, and a 20-year-old female domestic servant born in Badlesmere.

In **1891**, the Bentons were in residence. The make-up of this extended family is shown above on the census return for that year under Trimworth Farm (Table 10).

A sad footnote concerning the Benton family is found in the Godmersham burial records for August 1893 which show that James Benton, listed in the census as being 73, was killed on the railway only two years after the census date.

The **1901** census records a new tenant, Walter Gibbons, who was a farm manager of the Earl of Leicester's estate at Holkham Hall in Norfolk. At some stage he had married Anne from Wye, and together they had produced three sons and three daughters, all born at Wells in Norfolk. Since coming to Trimworth they had two more daughters and one son. In 1901 these nine children ranged in age from one to 20, with John, aged 16, being employed as a stockman on the farm. Incidentally, the census of 1901 records the number of houses with fewer than five rooms in the parish. This has been used by researchers as an indicator of poverty or social status. In 1901 Crundale parish recorded 29 (56 per cent) of its 52 houses as having fewer than five rooms.

This census information for Trimworth gives a good impression of what the census records can reveal. During the period under consideration (1841-1901), Trimworth was under the ownership of the Filmer family who appointed farm managers to supervise their estate. As can be seen, there was a fairly frequent turnover of farm managers, which means that the continuity in family inheritance usually seen in owner-occupied property is less apparent. However, the census has clearly proved to be a wonderful source of information for household occupancy, family relationships, ages and marital condition, occupational status, place of birth and characteristics of the farm economy such as farm size and labour force. It is therefore a key resource for the house historian.

Accessing census returns

There are three main sources:

1. Local record offices and reference libraries generally have copies of the census for the local area. County record offices will probably have them on micro-film or micro-fiche, with the facility for copying relevant pages. For the availability of these returns at the local level, see J. Gibson and E. Hampson, *Census Returns 1841 to 1891 in Micro-form: a directory to local holdings in Great Britain*, Family Records Centre, 1994.

2. The local Church of Jesus Christ of Latter Day Saints' Family History Centres will borrow micro-films from their headquarters in Utah to cover any part of the census you request. For locations of these libraries and access to the catalogue, visit www.familysearch.org.

3. The National Archives allows free online access to the census records from 1841 to 1911. There is a charge for printing paper copies. (www.nationalarchives.gov.uk/census)

ELECTORAL LISTS

The main use of these lists is to track the occupiers of a particular property. New family names appear as people move on or die. New entries of the same surname indicate that young people have reached voting age.

Before 1832, when the compilation of Electoral Registers began, **poll books** listed those who had voted in elections, and also how they voted, but they provide scant information on who lived where. The earliest records date from the end of the 17th century, when the right to vote was linked to the holding of freehold property worth 40 shillings or more. They really amount to a list of freeholders, but often fail to provide a precise address. Collections of Poll Books are held at the following locations:

1. Guildhall Library, Aldermanbury, London EC2 P2EJ. Tel.: 0207 3321868, www.cityoflondon.gov.uk

2. Institute of Historical Research, University of London, Senate House, WC1 E7HU Tel.: 0207 8628740, www.ihrinfo.ac.uk

3. Society of Genealogists, 14 Charterhouse Buildings, Goswell Road, EC1 M7BA. Tel.: 0207 2518799 www.sog.org.uk

From 1832, more comprehensive lists were produced of those entitled to vote, together with details of the property that gave them this entitlement, usually men owning land worth £10 or more. In 1867, this countryside qualification was dropped to £5, while all householders in towns were allowed to vote. In 1918 the right to vote was extended to all males over 21 and women householders over 30. The lists were now more comprehensive, and gave better details of properties. Further change occurred in 1928 when women were enfranchised and listings included street names and house numbers. The registers are usually arranged by street, and not by surname, as was the case before 1918.

Current electoral registers are held in district council offices, and local libraries will hold older records.

Electoral registers can also be searched online at http://www.eroll.co.uk/ They hold current and historical records for the UK, and records are constantly updated. Unlimited searches will cost £9.95 (tel.: 02920 474129)

The UK Electoral Roll can also be searched at www.theukelectoralroll.co.uk, where a one-house search by full name will cost £3.25.

Comprehensive information on these sources is provided by: J. Gibson and C. Rogers, *Electoral Registers since 1832 and Burgess Rolls*, Federation of Family History Societies (1990).

TRADE DIRECTORIES

Street and trade directories are another source for researching the sequence of occupiers. Many houses in the past were used to carry on various trades, and

43   **Kelly's Directory, Crundale and Godmersham, 1878.**

KENT.

CRUNDALE (or CRUNDALL) is a parish in the Eastern division of the county, lathe of Shepway, Wye hundred, East Ashford union, Ashford county court district, West Bridge rural deanery and archdeaconry and diocese of Canterbury, 3½ miles north-east from Wye station, 70 from London, 8 south-west from Canterbury, and 7 north-east from Ashford. The church of St. Mary stands upon elevated ground, three-quarters of a mile from the village, surrounded by trees, and consists of a chancel and nave, with a tower and steeple. The register dates from the year 1654. The living is a rectory, yearly value £375, with residence, in the gift of Sir Edmund Filmer, bart. and held by the Rev. Walter Arnold Vaughan, M.A. of Christ Church, Oxford, and domestic chaplain to Viscount Barrington. The Earl of Winchelsea holds a portion of the rectorial tithes. A fair is held yearly, on Whit Monday, for toys and pedlery. The charities for distribution amount to £35 yearly. Sir E. Filmer, bart. is lord of the manor of Trimworth, in this parish. The principal landowners are Sir E. Filmer, bart. E. Knight, esq. and J. S. W. S. E. Drax, esq. M.P. The soil is light; subsoil, chalk. The chief crops are corn and hops. The area is 1,587 acres; rateable value, £1,561; and the population in 1871 was 257.

SOLE STREET, 1 mile east, and DANEORD, half a mile north-west, are hamlets of this parish.

Parish Clerk, Richard Stacey.

POST OFFICE.—Thomas Smith Pilcher, receiver. Letters arrive from Canterbury at 9.30 a.m.; dispatched at 5.15 p.m. The nearest money order office is at Wye

National School, William Neal, master

Vaughan Rev. Walter Arnold, M.A. [rector]
Watts Rev. James, M.A. [curate]
Gambrill Austin, farmer

Page James, farmer
Pilcher Samuel, *Compasses*
Pilcher Thomas Smith, grocer
Richardson James, butcher

Stickles Charles, farmer
Sutton John, farmer
Warden Alfred, farmer

GODMERSHAM is a village and parish in the Eastern division of the county, lathe of Shepway, hundred of Felborough, union of East Ashford, Ashford county court district, Bridge rural deanery, and archdeaconry and diocese of Canterbury, 2 miles south-west from Chilham railway station, and 6 north from Ashford: it lies in the beautiful valley of the Stour, that stream passing through it in its course from Ashford to Canterbury, and on the high road from the former to the latter. The church of St. Lawrence is a Norman building, consisting of chancel, nave, south aisle and tower: the church was restored and enlarged and the interior decorated in 1865. Earliest date of register, 1564. The living is a vicarage, yearly value £234, with residence, in the gift of the Archbishop of Canterbury, and held by the Rev. Joshua Wilkinson, of St. Aidan's. Finch's charity of £30 yearly is for six poor labourers; other charities, of £12 yearly, are distributed. Godmersham House and Park is the seat of John Cunliffe Kay, esq. J.P: the park is large, and well stocked with deer. Chilham Park is on the north, and some long woods on the west. John Cunliffe Kay, esq. J.P. is lord of the manor and principal landowner. The soil is light; subsoil, chalk. The chief crops are wheat, beans and hops. The area is 3,077 acres; rateable value, £5,033 5s. and the population in 1871 was 393

POPE STREET is three quarters of a mile north-east; BILTING, 1 mile south-west; EGGERTON, 1 mile east, on the border of the great wood called Penny-Pot Wood.

Sexton, William Kennett Boys.

POST OFFICE.—William Kennett Boys, receiver. Letters received from Canterbury at 7.10 a.m.; dispatched at 6.40 p.m.; sundays, 10.25 a.m. The nearest money order office is at Wye

National School, Charles Vincer, master; Mrs. Caroline Vincer, mistress

Kay John Cunliffe, J.P. Godmersham pk
Knight Capt. William Wyndham, J.P. Bilting house
Wilkinson Rev. Joshua [vicar], Vicarage
Boughton Thomas, bricklayer

Boys William Kennett, grocer
Buss Horace Tylden, farmer
Epps Lewis, farmer
Gibbs William, shopkeeper
Hobday Richard, farmer

Stanford Charles, boot maker
Suttie James, land agent to John Cunliffe Kay esq. J.P. Estate office
Walker Thomas, blacksmith
Wills James Thomas, carpenter

44 *Kentish Express*, 3 October 1891.

KENTISH EXPRESS AND ASHFORD NEWS, OCTOBER 3, 1891.

EIGHT STACKS DESTROYED AT GODMERSHAM.

Between seven and eight o'clock on Wednesday evening the heavens in the direction of Chilham were lighted up with a dull red glare, caused by a fire at Trimworth Manor Farm, at Godmersham, occupied by Mr. James Benton, sen. Soon after eight o'clock an alarm was received at the Ashford Fire Brigade Station, and the engine was soon on the road. On arrival at the scene of the disaster it was found that two wheat stacks, two oat stacks, two barley stacks, two straw stacks, and one hay rick, all close together, were in full blaze, while in dangerous proximity to the burning stacks were several large barns and outhouses, as well as Mr. Benton's dwelling house. The efforts of the firemen were greatly impeded by the scarcity of water, none being obtainable within a few hundred yards. There were no hopes of saving the corn and straw stacks, as they were fully ablaze, and the efforts of the firemen were principally directed to the hay rick, most of which they managed to save, and to preventing the spread of the flames to the farm buildings and house. The brigade were able to leave for Ashford soon after six, as no further danger was apprehended, although flames were still issuing from the mass of burned *débris*. Mr. Benton was insured in the Kent Office, the damage being estimated at from £900 to £1,000. Great praise is due to the Ashford firemen, who, under Captain Hart, worked most assiduously and untiringly to put out the flames, even when it was seen to be utterly useless to attempt to save the stacks. Several of the Chilham brigade were present and lent valuable aid. Mr. Benton, jun., was in Ashford that evening for the purpose of engaging men to assist in thrashing out the corn stacks, and his first intimation of the fire was the arrival of the telegram for the brigade. The cause of the outbreak is unknown, but everything seems to point towards incendiarism. Mrs. Benton, we regret to hear, was lying dangerously ill at Trimworth Manor at the time.

the directories provide useful information on the location and nature of these trades people. Nationally, **Kelly's Directories** were produced from the middle of the 19th century for most communities, giving a street-by-street sequence of occupiers and any trade that was carried on at the house. Larger towns had much larger directories and even maps, although many of these have been subsequently removed. The content for villages is less comprehensive and it is not always easy to relate the trade described to a specific property. They exist, therefore, as useful supplementary information to land tax assessments and they are effective when used in conjunction with census returns. The 1878 Kelly's Directory for Kent gives an entry for Crundale and Godmersham which is reproduced here (Table 11). The best source for Kelly's Directories is the local library or county record office. Some are available online. The University of Leicester has a website for directories covering the period 1750 to 1920, www.historicaldirectories.org.

Several companies now produce directories and maps on CD, such as Archive CD books, 01594 829870, www.archivedbooks.org.

Antiquarian booksellers in your local region are another source, as is eBay.

See also G. Shaw and A. Tipper, *British Directories, a bibliography and guide to directories published in England and Wales 1850-1950*, Leicester University Press (1997).

Newspapers

Local newspapers are useful for property sales, and also for reporting incidents including deaths. An illustration of this is the great fire at Trimworth, reported in the *Kentish Express* and *Ashford News* on 3 October 1891 (Table 12). Trimworth was in the news a year later when another barn caught fire and was put out despite the brigade being hampered by lack of water. Most local newspapers date from the mid-19th century and are available in local archives and libraries. Some newspapers have their own archive collection and may even be indexed. The best collection of national and local newspapers is the British Library Newspaper Collections at Collindale Avenue, Collindale, London, NW9 5HE, Tel.: 0207 4127353, www.bl.uk/collections/newspapers.html. Their catalogue has entries for over 52,000 newspaper and periodical titles.

Conclusion

The sources covered in this chapter take us through to the Victorian period and into the 20th century. Because census information is 'closed' for a period of 100 years to protect confidentiality, the 1901 returns, released in 2002, are the latest currently available to the house historian. This is just one problem in accessing sources for the 20th century. Others include the impact of world wars in disrupting record collection and destroying records; population growth and mobility which has led to complications in tracing the line of owners in directories of various kinds; and the Law of Property Act 1925, which repealed copyhold tenure, resulting in the demise of many manorial estates and ending the centuries-old practice of manorial courts, described in Chapter 10. These problems explain why information on Trimworth Manor becomes less plentiful and more patchy since the house was sold by Sir Robert Marcus Filmer in 1911. Fortunately, other sources have helped to address the problem such as good continuity in Ordnance Survey mapping, detailed in Chapter 12, and the value of local and oral history.

CHAPTER 9

The Evidence of Property Ownership & Inheritance

PROPERTY INHERITANCE AND WILLS

Wills are an important way of tracking the movement of property, as well as providing an insight into family relationships and the prized property possessions of people living in the house. The will is a legal document in which the deceased person leaves instructions for the distribution of their property or estate. In order to ensure the validity of a will, it had to be proved in court and a probate granted so that requests could be paid. The probate was a guarantee that the will really was the last wishes of the deceased concerning the inheritance of property and possessions. Inheritance of land generally followed the common law (eldest son inherits, or if there are no sons, daughters share all). Generally, the better off were more likely to make a will because they had something to pass on.

Despite their value to the house historian, wills can be difficult to locate and use. They are private documents, and not necessarily deposited in the public domain. They may be fragile and difficult to read. Most old wills were written in Latin, although the use of English gradually increased so that by the 1700s only a few were in Latin. Frequently, the will may contain amusing personal insights that stand out from the formal legal instructions, such as the greengrocer who left £10 to his younger brother, 'for a new barrow to be built by Mr Hales East Street Sittingbourne', or a bookseller in Cambridge who left the house to his wife on condition she did not rent it to students, 'for undergraduate lodgers are more like hogs and wolves than human beings'. These examples, and others, are quoted from a helpful pamphlet written by Audrey Collins and produced by the Federation of Family History Societies, entitled 'Using Wills after 1858'. Another very helpful guide to the use of wills (mainly for family historians) is K. Grannum's booklet 'Using Wills', Public Records Office (2001).

The content of wills, illustrated with reference to
Sir Robert Filmer of Trimworth

The contents of wills vary but most are likely to contain a preamble, charitable bequests, provision for the widow and provision for children. In addition there are small bequests made for valuable items, such as jewellery or other objects of sentimental value. To illustrate some of this content, reference will now be made to the will of Sir Robert Filmer of East Sutton, who owned Trimworth Manor.

The will was made 'This seventeenth day of August in the second year of the reigne of our Sovereign Lady Anne by the Grace of God of England the Queen Defender of the Faith Anno Domini 1703.' (PROB11/574, available online, from the National Archives.)

The opening paragraph of the preamble also states 'this my last Will and testament', although this does not always mean that a will had been previously made. There is also a religious tone to the preamble in which Sir Robert asks to 'resign my soul unto the hands of Almighty God whose mercy for the sake and merits and of my Lord and Saviour Jesus Christ I humbly implore on his behalf'. As is common, Sir Robert also requests that he should be buried at the local church, in this case East Sutton. A bequest is made 'unto the poor of the Parish of East Sutton the sum of £5 to be distributed between them within three months next after my decease'. Sir Robert's provision for his widow contains some unusual content: 'unto my most dearly beloved wife Dame Elizabeth Filmer I give all my broad pieces of gold wheresoever and whatsoever and also my cart and one pair of cart horses for the use thereof'. His wife and eldest son inherit 'all my plate jewels, household stuff, stock of corn, hay goods, and chattels whatsoever and wheresoever equally to be divided between them share and share alike'.

As was common, the estate passed to the eldest son, including in this case the parsonage and rectory, 'and two pieces of meadow lyeing without the wall of my park at East Sutton paying there out yearly the value of twenty shillings in wheat or twenty shillings in money at Christmas to be then equally divided among eight of the poorest of the inhabitants of East Sutton'. Sir Robert's nephews and nieces were also rewarded with money, 'for their advancement', to be held by their parents, noting that they 'admit no opportunity that shall offer itself for the advancement of my said nephews and nieces in putting them out to trades or otherwise disposing of them as my said Wife and son shall think proper'. Unfortunately, this particular will gives little information about the houses or individual cottages and their rooms, but there are useful insights into the family, its wealth and social status, land and property.

PROBATE INVENTORIES

Inventories were sometimes taken shortly after the death of a person in order to protect the interests of beneficiaries. The inventory was also a protection for executors against any claims of fraud. These inventories were in the form of a list of personal effects and their value. They did not include land and property, although values of leases and mortgages were included. Often the inventory included the contents of each room in the house, allowing the house historian a chance to gain a clear insight into lifestyles and domestic arrangements. If these inventories can be obtained for a sequence of occupation of the house, then we can perceive changes in society, economic habits, household trends and living standards. Regional contrasts may also be observed if probate inventories can be sampled over a wider geographical area. A good example of the use of inventories is provided by M.W. Barley in his

Table 11: Richard's Probate Inventory of January 1694.
Inventory of Richard Camill, gentleman, appraised by Edward Croft, Francis Casmore and Francis Clayton, 17 January 1693[/4].

	£	s	d
His wearing apparrell and money in his purse.	10	0	0
In his Bedchamber - One bedstead, a feather bed and boulster, two pillowes, a paire of blankets and a coverlid, six cheires, two stools, one blanket, two glasses, one paire of andirons, a fire shovell and tongues, and a paire of bellowes.	6	18	0
In the Chamber over the Kitchen - Two bedsteads, two featherbeds and boulsters, a rug and two paire of blankets with a sett of curtaines and vallance, a chest of drawers, two trunks, two boxes, a table, two chaires, two lookeing glasses, a cradle, a great bible and severall other bookes.	9	6	0
In another Chamber - One trunck, one paire of Holland sheets, foure paire of flaxen sheets, foure paire of hempen sheets, three table cloaths, two dozen hempen napkins, foure paire of pillow drawers, a daiper table cloath and one dozen of daiper napkins.	7	0	0
In another Chamber - Wheat and rye, a parcell of chese, one paire of bucketts and some other implements	8	15	0
Twelve pound of yarne		16	0
In the Cockloft - One paire of bucskins, two paire of doe skins, a bedstead, a flockbed, a boulster, three blankets, two spinning wheels, a parcell of woollen yarne, a still and severall other implements.	3	18	0
In the Parlour - Two tables, six leather chaires, foure other chaires, a paire of andirons, fire shovell and tongues.	2	0	0
In the Kitchen - Three brasse kettles, two brasse potts, three skellets, a warming pan and a fryeing pan.	2	10	0
Seaven pewter dishes, a cheese plate, a pye plate, two dozen of trenchers and plates, three fowling peeces and a jack.	2	10	0
Two spitts, a dripping pan, a paire of racks, a paire of andirons, fire shovell & tongues, pot hookes and hangers.		15	0
Foure chaires, a bacon rack, two tressel boards, a chopping knife, a cleaver and two tables.		10	
In the Dayryhouse - A cheese presse, six barrells, two tubs, a churne, two kimnells, three pales, a dough cover (kiver), a trencher rack & 3 dozen of trenchers.	1	10	0
2 Flitchens of bacon.	1	0	0
Six milch cowes, 5 heifers, 2 calves.	42	0	0
One mare or nag and a filly.	13	6	8
Thirteene sheepe.	6	10	0
Eleaven lambs.	3	6	0
One hogg.	2	0	0
A parcell of oats in the barne.	2	10	0
A rick of hay and hay in the barne.	7	0	0
Three acres of corne growing on the land.	4	10	0
Nine silver spoons.	3	0	0
Implements & other things forgotten.		5	0
Debts sperate and desperate.	201	0	0
Total	**343**	**15**	**8**

Source: *Documenting the History of Houses*, N.W. Alcock, British Records Museum (2003). Archives and the User, No. 10, p.96.

1961 study *The English Farmhouse and Cottage*. The value of probate inventories for the study of an individual house is illustrated in a fascinating case study, published in N.W. Alcock's *Documenting the History of Houses* (2003). The case study involves the probate inventory of Richard Cahill of Stareton Warwickshire, who died in 1693, and the room-by-room contents are so detailed that it allows a virtual reconstruction of the house with all its fixtures and fittings (Table 13).

THE SOURCE OF WILLS AND INVENTORIES FOR HOUSE STUDY

Until 1858, all wills had to be proved (formally approved) by the Ecclesiastical Courts. This was called the Grant of Probate. There were two such courts known as **Prerogative Courts** (PC), one for the province of York, the other for the province of Canterbury. The Prerogative Court for York covered the counties of York, Durham, Northumberland, Westmoreland, Cumberland, Lancashire, Cheshire, Nottingham and the Isle of Man. The Prerogative Court of Canterbury (PCC) covered the rest of England and Wales. Many pre-1858 wills can be found in the county record offices, which may also have indexes. (See J. Gibson and E. Churchill, *Probate Jurisdictions, Where to look for Wills*, Federation of Family History Societies, 2002. This publication will give information on will indexes held at county record offices.) Both the Centre for Kentish Studies and the Canterbury Cathedral Archives have microform indexes. The person's name will usually be found under the year that probate was granted and it may be necessary to look a year or two after the date of death, because it may have taken time to complete the registration. Wills proved before the Prerogative Council of Canterbury for the period 1388 to 1858 can also be found in the National Archives, under Series PROB 11. They can also be searched online at www.documentsonline.nationalarchives.gov.uk and can be downloaded at a cost of £3.50 each. Three other sources for the indexes of wills for the Prerogative Court of Canterbury, usually on micro-film, are:

1. Society of Genealogists, 14 Charterhouse Buildings, Goswell Road, London, EC1M 7BA, Tel.: 0207 2518799, www.sog.org.uk

2. The Genealogical Society of Utah, British Isles Family History Service Centre, 185 Penns Lane, Sutton Coldfield, West Midlands B76 8JU, www.familysearch.com

Records for the Prerogative Court of York are at the Borthwick Institute, University of York, Heslington, YO10 5DD. Tel.: 01904 321166, www.york.ac.uk/inst/bihr

After 1858, probate jurisdiction was shifted from the church to a new secular Court of Probate. This central location means that they are easier to search. They are indexed annually and available on micro-fiche. Once again it is advisable to search over a period of two or three years from the date of death, and even longer in cases where the estate is disputed. Copies of wills and administrations can be ordered by post from the Principal Registry of the Family Division, First Avenue House, 42-9 High Holborn, London, WC1V 6NP. www.hmcourts-service.gov.uk

Copies of the wills cost £5.00 either to view or to be posted to you. Postal searches also cost £5.00 for a four-year search period, plus a copy of the will. First Avenue House is on the north side of High Holborn, mid-way between Chancery Lane and Holborn underground station. Indexes for 1858 to 1943 are to the left of the Search Room, and for 1944 onwards to the right. Facilities for visitors at First Avenue House are very good. There are eight micro-fiche readers for searching the most recent indexes.

Finally, a Name Index for the period 1858 to 1943 is available on micro-fiche at both the National Archives and the Family Records Centre.

Probate Inventories are generally available for the period 1660 to 1750, but some go back to 1539, the year they were introduced. It is the inventory that is probably more valuable to the house historian (and less so to the family historian), but unfortunately they are less extensively indexed. For the period 1660-1750 see P. Spufford (ed.), *Index to the Probate Accounts of England and Wales*, British Record Society, vols 12 and 13 (1999). It is likely that many county record offices will have their own Probate Inventories.

TITLE DEEDS AND THE RECORD OF PROPERTY OWNERSHIP

The title deed is a record of property transfer and can be one of the most important documents, giving evidence about the house, its owners and occupiers and the use of land. In order to sell a property you had to have evidence that you were entitled to sell it, and this evidence came in the form of a property deed. There was no systematic registration of land or property transfers until the Land Registry was formed in 1862. Until that time, title deeds and transfers of land and property were handled by courts of law, although the system varied depending on type of property and the time of transfer, making the search somewhat complicated.

Having been found, the property deeds may still present problems to the researcher. As legal documents, they contain a great deal of jargon and can be extremely repetitive and hard to read. Frequently the house deeds form part of a package which includes indentures, mortgages, wills and manorial records. Do not be put off by these potential difficulties, because the search is invariably rewarding, giving the house historian valuable information on the names of vendors and purchasers, a description of the land and property, dates of transfer and family relationships. It is possible that maps will be included, especially after 1840.

The content of title deeds with particular reference to Trimworth Manor

Anyone reading a title deed will be aware of the plethora of legal jargon which has to be cut through to find items of real interest. Fortunately, there are standard structures to these documents which allow the reader to pinpoint the important areas of ownership, property description, etc. (Table 14).

Deeds seldom give the date that the property was built. Occasionally there are references to 'new built' or 'late built' but these phrases can be repeated in successive deeds, often decades after the house has been built. Detailed descriptions of houses

Table 12: Clauses in post-medieval deeds.
The phrases are usually more repetitive than shown here, e.g. an action clause might read 'hath, granted, bargained, sold, released, and confirmed, and doth grant, sell, release and confirm'.

Clause	Text	Comments and Significance
Introduction	This Indenture tripartite	Bipartite (2), quadripartite, etc., depending on the number of parties.
Date	dated the	
Parties	Between ... of the first part and ... of the second part, etc.	The people concerned. One party may consist of several people.
	Witnesseth that	
Recital	Whereas ...	Describes previous transactions, sometimes very numerous.
	Now the said ...	'Now' ends the recital.
Consideration	for and in consideration of ...	Often the actual sum of money; sometimes a cautious 'for good and sufficient consideration' or 'for natural love and affection; 5s for minor parties.' The end of the recital may explain how the consideration was paid.
Action	doth demise (lease) or grant or release or assign ... unto ...	These are the main alternatives though each is wrapped up in many more words.
Property	All that messuage ... together with all ways watercourses, ...	The property involved. Such inclusive clauses do not mean that property included any watercourses, etc., but guard against any omissions.
	(and also ...)	Another property, or something like a right of way.
	together with all title deeds ...	Alternatively 'such deeds as relate solely' to the property.
	To have and to hold the said messuage ... to the said ... his heirs and assigns ...	
Period	For the term of ... (or) For ever	Distinguishes between a permanent grant and one for a limited period, long or short.
Tenure	To be holden of the chief lord ...	Not always included. A medieval survival that can be ignored.
Rent	Yielding and paying ...	The rent, if any.
Uses	to the use of the said ...	Who benefits - this clause can be very complex.
Conditions and Covenants	Subject to ...	By far the most variable clause with both formal and significant covenants.
	and the said ...	
	further covenanteth ...	
Warranty	And the said ... warranteth that he hath not done any action ...	A restatement of the right of the seller to the property.
Witness	In witness whereof the said ... hath hereunto set his name and seal the day and year above written	
Back surface (dorse) and endorsements		Carries the witnesses to the signing, sometimes with receipts and additional memoranda, sometimes including the texts of complete deeds. A summary is often written (endorsed), on the surface exposed when the deed is folded up.

Source: *Documenting the History of Houses*, N.W. Alcock, British Records Museum (2003). Archives and the User, No. 10, p.28.

are quite rare, generally referring to out-buildings, such as barns and stables, and giving information on the farmland. The value of these descriptions is that they give an impression of the economic status of the house, and the social standing of its occupants.

The Centre for Kentish Studies contains good records on title deeds which refer to Trimworth, often as part of the deeds of East Sutton, the main residence of the Filmer family, who also owned Trimworth. Records exist from 1607 and at intervals through to the mid-19th century. The earliest document is a land conveyance of 1607, the date of the death of Sir Thomas Kempe, who had inherited Trimworth in 1558. On his death the manor passed to Reginald Kempe. The document (Fig. 43) is an alienation, or transfer of property away from the normal line of inheritance, creating a use of part of the estate to Edmund Randolph. This gift of land received royal assent as confirmed by the great seal of James I.

Another document of greater significance is the record described as 'Title Deeds, Trimworth, and the Advowson of Crondell passing to Filmer family on marriage of Dorothy Tuke to Robert Filmer 1649'.

For many years, Trimworth had been in the hands of the Kempe family, most recently Reginald Kempe, who died in 1612. His wife died five years later, and

45   Land transfer, Trimworth, 1607.
The date coincides with the inheritance of Trimworth by Sir Reginald Kempe. This document is an alienation, or transfer of a piece of land away from the normal line of inheritance. It has royal assent as indicated by the seal of James I. (Reproduced with permission of the Kent Archive Service and the Centre for Kentish Studies.)

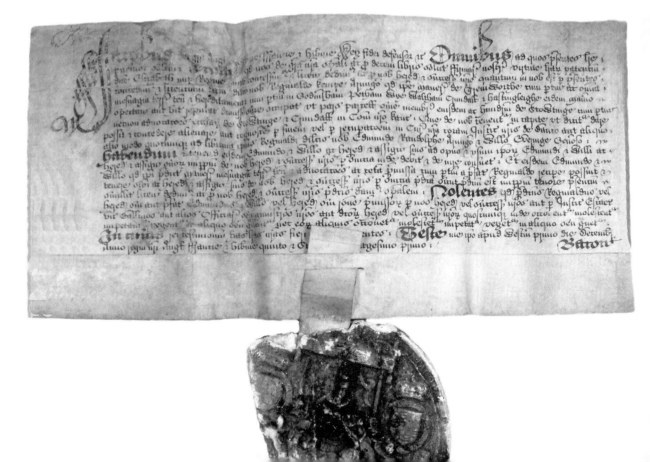

Trimworth eventually passed to daughter Amy, who had married Morris Tuke. Their only daughter carried the inheritance in 1649 on marriage to Robert Filmer. The deeds relate to this significant event which led to Trimworth being transferred into Filmer hands for the next 260 years. Dorothy Tuke is described as being 'of the Sittie of Westminster in the Countie of Middlesex, spinster cousin and now heir of Thomas Kempe late of Trimworth'. Robert Filmer is introduced as 'of the sittie of Westminster, gentleman, second son of Sir Robert Filmer of East Sutton in the Countie of Kent'. The document then uses the familiar words 'witnessieth that … ' and goes on to announce the marriage between Dorothy and Robert, and the property which now passes into the hands of Robert. The phrase 'all that … ' is a sign that the deed will now list the property involved:

> the capital messuage [property] of the Manor house of Tremworth afor said and all the singular messuage houses edifices buildings barns stables dovecotes gardens orchards curtaliges crofts tofts arable lands meadow pastures closures wood underwoods hoaths firzes moors marshes pools water and watercourses commons commons of pasture fishing fowling hawking hunting.

The document refers also to the extremely important right of patronage of the parish church of 'Crondall' (Crundale) in which is enshrined the right of the lord of the manor to appoint the vicar (i.e., the advowson).

We can also gain good information on Trimworth Farm, which contained 50 acres of meadow, 350 acres of pasture, 150 acres of wood and 250 of land (presumably arable). This total of 760 acres must have made Trimworth 'and its appurtenances in Crondall, Bodsham, Godmersham, Waltham and [Ruckinge?]' one of the principal manorial estates in the area, which now was to grow and prosper further under the ownership of successive Filmers until 1910.

Finding title deeds

Today when people purchase a property, they usually apply for a mortgage and the title deeds for that property are deposited with the mortgage provider or solicitor as security. Therefore the search for the modern title deeds should begin with the bank, building society or solicitors acting on behalf of the mortgage provider. They will generally charge a fee for viewing. Once the mortgage has been paid, you are entitled to claim your title deeds, thus many deeds pass into private hands and often become inaccessible. When compulsory registration of all property transactions with the Land Registry began in 1990, old deeds were legally superseded (see below). In order to save space, many building societies disposed of them in a bin or returned them to the current property owner, or occasionally deposited them with the county record office. The result of this is that all too frequently we have lost many years of detailed history on home ownership.

Some county record offices will have catalogues of title deeds, but records of older properties will vary according to whether the property has a distinctive name, or some local status as a manor house or part of a larger estate. The search for Trimworth

Manor at the Centre for Kentish Studies revealed property deeds dated back to 1649, but this was an unusual and unexpected find. Even more unusual was the fact that the deeds were legible, although the documents required very careful handling. The National Archives contain many title deeds, especially for properties which formed part of a large estate, or which at some time resorted to the Crown through purchase or forfeiture. Some of these will have been described and indexed in *A Descriptive Catalogue of Ancient Deeds in the Public Records Office*, six volumes, HMSO, available in the Reading Room at the National Archives. Two texts which give greater detail on this aspect of house research are: N.W. Alcock, *Old Title Deeds: A Guide for Local and Family Historians* (Phillimore, 2001), and N. Barratt, *Tracing the History of Your House*, 2nd edn, National Archives (2006), Ch. 5.

The National Land Registry

The Land Registry was established in 1862 in order to record land transfers. Up to that point most transactions were not officially recorded. Initially, the system was piecemeal, voluntary and rarely used, but in 1899 it was made compulsory for London. Slowly the system spread to other towns and cities, but it was not made compulsory everywhere in England and Wales until 1990. Presently about 70 per cent of all eligible properties are actually covered by the Land Registry records, a figure that will grow as more properties come on to the register. Land Register Online provides easy access to details of more than 20 million properties in England and Wales and can be accessed between 7.00 a.m. and 12 midnight, Monday to Saturday. There is a cost of £3.00 for each property detail, and an additional £4.00 for each title plan. Fees are payable online. The information provided gives details of the property, ownership, price (if registered since 1 April 2000), rights of way and covenants. The address is www.landregistry.gov.uk/wps/portal/property_search.

CHAPTER 10

Manorial and Estate Records

The manorial records for Trimworth are perhaps the most valuable resource available in studying the history of the estate and its use over a long period. The records give us a comprehensive and fascinating insight into the organisation and management of the land, and the everyday lives of a host of tenants. Disputes, abuses and offences are described in detail, such as problems of overgrazing, cultivating common land, damage caused by straying animals and neglect of hedges. There is information on buildings within the estate together with names of residents and tenants, providing a sequential link over the generations. However, no historical records were collected for the convenience of the student of local history. Manorial records do not cover the whole of England because the manorial system was not applied uniformly across England and Wales. Neither are records always easy to read, because some early records will be in Latin; others will be in a form of English which is unfamiliar or heavily abbreviated. Despite these problems, this chapter will illustrate their value with specific reference to Trimworth. In order to appreciate their content and use, it is first necessary to review the manor and the systems of land tenure, leading on to a review of the holding of manor courts, and an assessment of their records.

THE MANOR AND THE MANORIAL SYSTEM OF LAND TENURE

'It is very difficult to provide an adequate definition of an institution which began to emerge before the Norman Conquest and which continued to function until the 20th century.' So begins the first chapter of *Using Manorial Records* by Mary Ellis, published by the Public Records Office in 1997, which has been helpful in compiling this background to the use of manorial records. The manor is usually considered to be a unit of land with the lord's residence (messuage), and a collection of tenants' dwellings surrounded by fields under cultivation. These fields would be in strips and shared out between the tenants. Land owned and farmed by the lord was known as demesne land. There were many variations on this 'ideal' form; often the lord would own several pieces of land which were not necessarily contiguous, but spread among land of other manors. 'Hence the concept of a manor as a compact geographical unit is in many ways less helpful and less meaningful than Norden's view of a manor as a system of social and economic organisation, based on tenants holding land from a superior Lord.' (Ellis, 1997, p.6)

This system of relationships between lords and tenants began before the Norman Conquest. Peasants enjoyed the protection of an influential figure, while the lord in return gained labour and payments. With the Norman Conquest came a significant change. William I began to reward his successful military figures with grants of large pieces of land, thus replacing Saxon nobility with the Norman equivalent (the 'tenants in chief'), although the everyday lives of people at the lower end of the social scale were largely unaffected by the change. The arrival of the Black Death in the second half of the 14th century also caused a significant change. Up to that time, manorial tenants were either 'free' (freeholders) or 'unfree' (villeins or bondmen), but the ravages of the Black Death caused a dramatic slump in population and cultivation, and the lords were unable to find enough tenants. This meant that the bargaining position of the villeins became stronger and they were able to demand greater security and personal freedoms. Gradually these villeins became the customary tenants or copyholders of land, because they agreed to abide by the customs of the manor and were given a copy of the agreement as proof of title. Copyholders or customary tenants (the terms are used interchangeably) became the most numerous in terms of numbers and amounts of land held.

Copyholders were either tenants for life, after which the land reverted to the lord, or tenants of inheritance, in which case they passed the land on to the eldest son (primogeniture), or, as was prevalent in Kent, to all sons (partible inheritance or gavelkind). The customary tenant usually made cash payments or gave labour services to the lord, and in addition paid an 'entry fine' upon becoming accepted as a customary tenant, usually equivalent to one or two years' rent. (These entry fines are recorded at each of the manor court meetings, along with other fees and fines.) Customary tenants were required to maintain buildings and hedges and keep the land in good condition, otherwise they could lose their holding.

Freeholders, unlike copyholders, were largely independent of the manorial system and were not subject to restrictions on their personal freedom. They could sell or dispose of their land without reference to the manorial courts. They paid a fixed rent to the lord and were usually required to attend the manor courts, possibly serving as jurors. On the death of a freeholder, the person purchasing or inheriting the land had to pay a relief to the lord, usually the equivalent of one year's rent.

There were two other kinds of tenant: leaseholders and tenants at will. Leaseholders took a tenancy for a fixed number of years, usually 21, which was considered long enough for the leaseholder to invest in the land and maintain it in good condition. Rents were regularly reviewed and could consist of payments in kind, such as hens or other livestock. Tenants at will, or cottars, were the poorest and most vulnerable. They were usually cottagers with a small garden, paying a small rent, and relying for their future on the goodwill of the lord. They rarely appear in the court records.

The administration of the manorial estate was undertaken by a number of officials, the chief officer being the steward. The steward acted for the lord and was supported by the bailiff, who administered the day-to-day running of the manor. A reeve was the official appointed to oversee the cultivation of land belonging to the lord, while the hayward supervised the making of hay and harvesting. There were variations in this structure, but the steward and bailiff were common to most manors and were largely responsible for the efficient administration of the manor and the manorial records.

THE MANOR COURT AND ITS RECORDS

> In 1641 Sir Edward Coke in the Compleat Copyholder said that the central Court of the Manor, the Court Baron 'is incident to and inseparable from, a manor … and is the chief Prop and Pillar of the Manor, for that no sooner faileth, but the Manor falleth to the Ground'. This quotation does two things. Firstly, it reinforces the idea established in Chapter 1, that the Manor was a social rather than a geographical concept and secondly, it emphasises the key role that the Courts played in the Manorial system.
>
> (Ellis, 1997, p.47)

As already stated, the steward and bailiff had a major role in the regulation of the manor's affairs including social and economic disputes. Meetings, called the manor courts, were held to address problems and review tenancies. Details of decisions were recorded in the Court Rolls, which date from the late 13th century. The Court Rolls for the Manor of Wye (in which some details of Trimworth Manor are also recorded) date from 1284 to 1409. The Court Rolls for Trimworth itself run from 1648 through to 1920, 'providing intriguing and informative glimpses of actual events in the day to day lives of manorial tenants' (Ellis 1998, p.47). To appreciate their true value to the house historian, it is necessary to briefly review the workings of the manorial court.

Significantly, the court represented a transfer of jurisdiction from royal courts to the manorial lord, which is why the records state that the court is being held in the name of the king. Manorial lords therefore might be granted important responsibilities, such as the right and responsibility to ensure that bread and ale were provided to a sufficient standard, and that short measures were not being sold. Proceedings of the court were written on parchment rolls (Court Rolls), and from the 16th century more commonly in a written volume or book. Latin was often used, then from the 16th century a mixture of English and Latin, before Parliament decreed in 1733 that all administrative records should be written in English. Since the business of all courts was similar, the records conformed to a set pattern. The following sequence of events defines the stages in the holding of the manor court.

1. The steward, who presides over the court, issues a precept to the bailiff of the manor giving notice that the court is to be held.

2. With the court assembled, the steward reads out details of those tenants unable to attend, and who have paid essoins (payment for not attending court, usually delivered by a proxy).

3. Tenants not in attendance for no given reason were liable to a heavier fine or amercement.

4. Selection of the jury is made, and the jury is sworn in.

5. A presentment was made by the jury on behalf of the tenants, stating the business of the meeting. This agenda was probably agreed some days before the meeting. Presentments may include all kinds of disputes, some petty, some serious.

6. The various transactions on tenancy involving copyhold or customary land would be decided upon, such as individuals surrendering their tenancy or being admitted to a tenancy. Often the change was the result of a death. This death would be announced then new tenants admitted. All these decisions would be recorded in the Court Manor Rolls, and a copy given to the individuals concerned, hence the term 'copyhold'.

The running of the court involved some professional expenses. A document in the Centre for Kentish Studies (U1397M1) gives details of correspondence between Sir Robert Filmer and his solicitor, Robert Hoar of Maidstone. A collection of invoices from Hoar to Filmer represents the costs to the steward in carrying out the court.

> **For Trimworth**, 1887
> November to December. **Professional charges** with reference to taking instructions for Court Baron, drawing lists of tenants and copies, preparing and despatching summonses to tenants, preparing precepts and advertising Court Baron, self and clerk and afterwards attendance correspondence to tenants of the Manor £3 9s. 4d.
> Out of pocket expenses £2 4s. 1d.
> Total £5 13s. 5d.

Sir Robert writes in turn to the solicitor 'to one who does not understand the details of the work required, the annual expenses charged (£5 13s. 5d.) are out of proportion to the amount received (£19 17s. 5d.)'. The solicitor then attempts to explain this by noting the number of letters and interviews necessary to do his job. A note of irritation is sounded, 'You can, of course have a full statement of all these interviews and letters and all the other professional work if you wish it: it would be a very lengthy document made up of a large number of small items.' For reassurance he adds, 'the charges are made out in the same way as they were in the late Sir Edward Filmer's lifetime, and on the same scale exactly'. This appears to be the final word on the matter.

THE COURT MANOR ROLLS FOR TRIMWORTH MANOR

There are two major sources. The first is the Court Rolls for the Royal Manor of Wye, which run from 1297 to 1409. The manors of Wye and Trimworth were adjoining, and were likely to have tenants with land in both manors, therefore the court business for Wye makes frequent reference to Trimworth ('Tremworth', 'Thermworthe'). The rolls deal with essoins (excuses for absence) of those who were chief tenants (probably those holding a yoke or more). Lesser tenants were listed separately. In the record for 1284, we see the appearance of Roger de Crondale, who is believed to have been a master mason responsible for building work in Crundale church (see *Guide to the Church of*

46   Knapped flint, Crundale church.
The work of Roger de Crundale, seen on the north and south walls of the chancel. The skilled flint knapping on the left contrasts with the use of irregular flints in the form of rubble to the right.

St Mary by Albert Lancefield). Roger had been a court mason at Westminster, and eventually retired to Crundale in 1297. He was a member of the School of Masons in Canterbury and London during the latter years of the 13th century. Some of his work can be seen in the external flint work of the north and south walls of the chancel, considered to be some of the finest knapped flint existing in Kent (Fig. 44). He was obviously a busy man, frequently being listed under the essoins for his absence, which was reported by his proxy, William Le Kake (of Kake's Yoke, now Hunt Street Farm in Crundale (Fig. 45).

47   Cakes Yoke, 2007 (a charcoal and pen sketch by the author).
*This splendid manor which retains many medieval features was held by John **Cake** who in 1312 had two **yokes**, a yoke being about 60 acres. It is now known as Hunt Street after the Hunte family, who had been resident in Crundale for more than five hundred years.*

The rolls refer to problems, such as flooding on the road between the properties of John de Handlo and Thomas Coumbe at Tremworth (1295), and an agreement reached in 1311 between Christian, wife of Stephen de Lombesfeld, and Trissina, wife of Thomas de Lombesfeld, 'following Trissina verbally insulting Christian and spreading stories about her family. Thomas puts himself into the Lord's hands.'

Theft of animals is a frequent occurrence. In 1372, Thomas Marchal was called to court to answer to John Lombisfelde for taking away a cow worth 13s. 4d. from a certain field (*campo*). Thomas defends himself by saying John is in arrears on rent. Six months later, William Town is accused of stealing 150 eggs worth four shillings from Richard de Lombesfeld, 'and took them away to his own premises without just cause'. John Lombesfeld is in the Manor Rolls again in 1373, this time complaining that John Carter had stolen one of his horses from Trimworth, and was keeping it in a field at Crundale, 'to the damage of 3s 4d'. Six months later the jury decided that since Lombesfeld owed two years' rent on Carter's mill, the horse should be kept until the debt was paid. In addition, Lombesfeld was fined sixpence for making a false claim!

These entries are records of day-to-day events and disputes in the running of the manorial estate. Other events include neglect of hedges, damage caused by straying animals, failure to clear ditches, theft of timber, encroaching on common land, etc. The documents are full of names of tenants and their relations, and are valuable as sources for the family historian as well as the house historian.

Court Rolls for Trimworth Manor, which run from 1648 to 1920

In 1648, Sir Robert Filmer married Dorothy Tuke and became Lord of the Manor at Trimworth. From that date a manor court was held through to 1910, when Sir Robert Marcus Filmer sold the estate. The court met on two further occasions, the last being in 1920. Throughout this period of 270 years, the court met to record rents, tenants, fines, summons, oaths, deaths, and occupiers of the manor. Each record of a meeting follows a similar format in the Court Rolls (Fig. 46).

1. The heading of the roll gives details of the type of court, names of manor, lord and steward, and the date of session. Names of jurors are then listed ('the homage'), and duly sworn in.

2 The presentments are then dealt with, including such matters as disputes between tenants, repairs to property, boundary disputes, etc. A good example is recorded in the Court Rolls for the year 1733, which reads as follows.

> It was agreed between Sir Edward Filmer and John Sawbridge Esquire that the said John Sawbridge shall repair all the hedges, gates bars and styles and all other fences that divide the woodlands and other lands lying in the Parish of Crundale belonging to the said Sir Edward Filmer now in the occupation of Thomas Page which abut and bound upon pasture land belonging to the said John Sawbridge of Olanteigh and the said John Sawbridge agrees to maintain a ditch 15 inches deep and 18 inches wide from the present forsake of the said

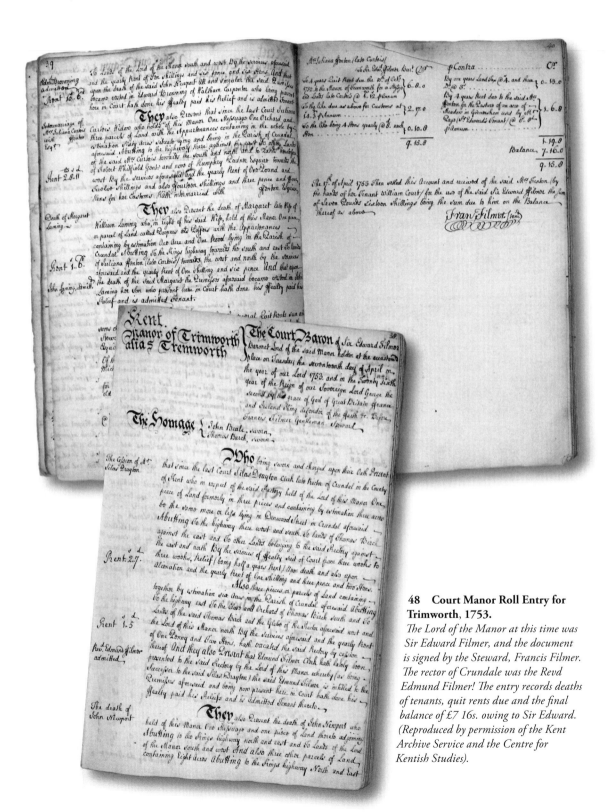

48 Court Manor Roll Entry for Trimworth, 1753.
The Lord of the Manor at this time was Sir Edward Filmer, and the document is signed by the Steward, Francis Filmer. The rector of Crundale was the Revd Edmund Filmer! The entry records deaths of tenants, quit rents due and the final balance of £7 16s. owing to Sir Edward. (Reproduced by permission of the Kent Archive Service and the Centre for Kentish Studies).

hedge and no further. In consideration of his having all the wood and trees that shall grow in the said hedges.

3. Administration of copyhold land now follows.

The death of tenants is recorded in the Court Roll, and the land technically surrendered back to the Lord. Then the new heir is announced, often being required to grasp an official rod held by the steward to mark formal admittance to the property (Fig. 47). The entry usually gave a full description of the newly acquired property and the relationship between deceased and new tenant.

It is impossible to feature the content of all the many courts that took place during the 270 years covered by the rolls for Trimworth Manor, but there are some high points of interest. In 1709 the steward's notes read:

> That every Tenant be summon'd by leaving a printed summons with him or at the House of the Tenant in Possession, for Warning Tenants by word of mouth do not answer the Purpose so well as a Printed Summons.

In 1733, the Steward pleads as follows:

> let it be remember'd that one day is not sufficient to keep the Courts for the Manors of Trimworth and Hinxell and receiving the rents and wood money. Therefore let the Dinner be divided into two, the first Day for the Tenants and the Woodman and the second for keeping the two Courts viz the first Tuesday and Wednesday in July.

(Remember, tenants were travelling from High Holden, Frittenden and Cranbrook as the manor's lands were so widely distributed, and a dinner was necessary for those travelling such long distances.) We even have the menu for the two meetings referred to above.

> Dinner at Trimworth the said Tuesday in July when there is no Court
> for Tenants or Woodman
> The menu is as follows:
> A Clod of Beef boyl'd with butter'd Carrets.
> A leg and shoulder of Mutton roasted
> Malt three Bushels.

> Court Dinner for the Tenants of Trimworth and Hinxell.
> Two bak'd suit Puddings with Raysons.
> One Clod of Beef boyl'd with Carrets.
> One SrLoyn or Rump of Beef roasted.
> One Loyn of Mutton bak'd in a Pye.
> Five Bushels of Malt.

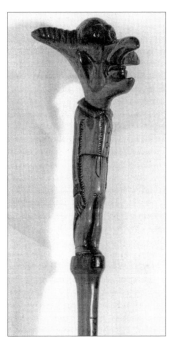

49   The Steward's Rod.
Such rods were used in the formal admission of customary tenants to the manor, in this case the Manor of Church Aston, Shropshire. (From M. Ellis, Using Manorial Records (PRO, 1994).

The Steward provides the following footnote: 'At a Court at Trimworth three bushels of malt are required and three bushels for the Tenants, if they are kept any distance time apart, but if kept together then five bushels will serve for both days.'

1920 was the last meeting of the Court Baron for Trimworth. There were just four tenants present: Lord Marsham, the Revd Ford, Frederick Warde and Mackeson and Company. In 1922, the Law of Property Act enfranchised all copyholders, and by 1926 the last pieces of copyhold land had been turned into freehold. So ended the operation of a landholding system that dominated the social and economic life of much of England and Wales from the Saxon period to the early 20th century. Where a long record of Court Barons exist, as in the case of Trimworth Manor, it is possible to reconstruct a long and at times colourful history of a house, its land and, of course, the people who inhabited it.

LOCATING MANORIAL RECORDS

As with many records of local history, the best place to begin a search is at the county record office. For example, at the Centre for Kentish Studies a card index of manors within the county is kept, together with a list of documents in the archives relating to that manor, including Court Manor Rolls where they exist. A Manorial Documents Register for the country was set up in 1926, following the abolition of Copyhold Tenure. This gives the manors known to have existed in a parish, and the records which survive. Occasionally, a problem can arise if the Court Baron lives outside the local area or even the county. (The Filmer family seat was East Sutton, although they held court for the the manors at Trimworth and several others throughout Kent.) The Manorial Documents Register is held at the National Archives. Several counties have been computerised and can be searched online. The remainder have been microfilmed and are available for consultation in the Map and Large Document Reading Room.

It is advisable to consult one of the succinct and clearly written Research Guides available at the National Archives, or on the internet. The three most useful are:

1. Manor and other local Court Rolls from the 13th century to 1922.

2. The Manorial documents register.

3. Manorial documents in the National Archives.

CHAPTER 11

The Use of Tax Records to Identify Owners and Occupiers

The thought of taxation records is unlikely to excite the house historian, probably because it brings to mind the annual chore of completing tax returns. However, governments have raised levies on land and property for centuries, and the records of these levies are useful in linking owners or occupiers with payments and responsibilities. They are most useful when used in combination with other historical sources, such as trade directories or electoral lists, because it is sometimes difficult to relate the tax records for a particular person to a specific address. Tax records can also help to explain sudden changes in architectural features of a house, especially those taxes that were based on a number of fixed features, such as windows or fire hearths. Property owners frequently bricked up windows or hearths in order to avoid payment, tax evasion being as common then as now!

LAND TAX

The land tax was a national tax raised in 1693 to replace a range of earlier taxes. A fixed sum of money was agreed and raised as a levy on each county. Local assessors then fixed quotas for each parish, to be paid by individual landowners. Unfortunately, the land tax boundaries do not always coincide with ecclesiastical parish boundaries. The tax was raised for the period 1693 to 1963 but most records survive from 1780, for a very good reason. In that year the right to vote was allocated to people with freehold property valued at £2 and upwards, so land taxes became synonymous with entitlement to vote and records took on an important role. After 1798, the tax could be commuted by a lump sum payment by the tenant, equivalent to 16 years' payment of tax. This explains the column in the returns which reads 'sums assessed and exonerated'. From this date, assessment forms contained rentals (value of property), name of proprietor, name of occupier (often the tenant), and name or description of property (this usually appears from 1825). For parishes with a tithe map, it is possible to link owners and occupiers with the land tax records, and where a sequence of land tax returns exist for a long period, it is interesting to trace continuity and change in owner occupiers.

Land tax records for Trimworth

These are available at the Centre for Kentish Studies from 1780 to 1787, then 1791, 1801, 1820 and 1831. An example of an assessment form is shown in Fig. 48. Note

50 Land tax assessment for the Borough of Trimworth, 1801.

The proprietors are listed, together with the occupiers of the land, and the land tax assessment in quarterly and yearly payments. Familial names appear, such as the Filmers, and Edward Austen, brother of Jane.

the administrative area for assessment is known as Trimworth Borough, and not Crundale parish. The list of proprietors reveals some interesting names. Sir Beversham Filmer had inherited Trimworth in 1797. The Revd Sir Edmund Filmer was vicar of Crundale and was to inherit Trimworth on the death of Sir Berversham in 1805. The Revd Sir Edmund married Annabella Honeywood, daughter of Sir John Honeywood, whose first wife's maiden name was Goodenough. The third name in the assessment list is Edward Austen, brother of Jane Austen. (The tax records for 1826 list him as Edward Knight, having changed his name on the inheritance from Mrs Knight of Godmersham Park.) Note the records do not show house name or number; neither do the payments give any reliable indication of personal wealth or fortune. Remember, the amount a parish paid was fixed in 1698, and this amount was then allocated proportionally to the rateable value of houses. The amount paid stayed the same for years. Trimworth Borough collected the same amount (£49 8s.) from 1780 until 1801. Where the amount for a single property increases suddenly, it is probably the result of renovation, or rebuilding or an extension, in which case the rateable value rose.

The availability of land tax returns

County record offices are the best places to begin a search, where it is likely that a separate list of tax returns is available, perhaps on micro-fiche or micro-film. For Kent, there is an extensive collection at the Centre for Kentish Studies, and the Canterbury Cathedral Archives hold records for the years 1752 to 1795. A very useful book on the survival and location of these records is: J. Gipson, M. Medleycott and D. Mills, *Land and Window Tax Assessments*, The Federation of Family History Societies (1998).

Hearth Tax

The hearth tax records 'give an unparalleled insight into the composition and nature of 17th-century communities, and provide a useful supplement to other local records such as Parish Registers'. This is the introduction to a *Research Guide on Domestic Records* (No. 32), National Archives, which has been used here to source information on this topic. The hearth tax was introduced in 1662 to help with serious financial problems facing the government of Charles II. The tax was finally repealed in 1689. Under the terms of the Act, the tax was paid by people whose house was worth more than 20s. a year, and who also contributed to local church and poor rates. It is not, therefore, a comprehensive census, because many were exempt under these terms. Each liable householder had to pay one shilling for each hearth within their property. Payments were due twice yearly, but the assessment and collection of the tax was complex and inconsistent. The best records are for the periods 1662-6, and 1669-74, when the tax was administered by royal officials. Outside these periods, the tax was contracted out to private collectors, and many of these returns do not survive. Privatisation of public services is not always the best solution!

Why a hearth tax? Firstly, many large 17th-century houses were being renovated and chimneys were being built to channel smoke through the roof. This is particularly true of the open-hall houses (such as Trimworth), where ceilings were being put in to give floors and more rooms, each of which required a new fireplace. Secondly, this was an exceptionally cold period, referred to by some as the Little Ice Age, and so more fires were needed to keep houses warmer. The tax was, not surprisingly, extremely unpopular, requiring inspectors to enter houses and check that returns were accurate. The idea was basically that the bigger the house, the more fireplaces, and therefore the more money available to pay the tax. Charitable institutions were exempt, as well as industrial hearths such as kilns and furnaces (but not smithies and bakeries). Grounds for exemption also included poverty of the residents, who were probably 'cottagers' with only one hearth.

Table 15 shows the hearth tax returns for the Borough of Trimworth, which were located at the Centre for Kentish Studies. A glance at the figures reveals an initial problem: the records list occupiers and not houses. It is unlikely to find any addresses in the hearth tax records. The records for Trimworth Borough were dated 1664, some fifty or sixty years after Trimworth Manor had been converted from a hall house to a house with two floors. The original hall would now consist of two rooms (two hearths), the original service wing, also two rooms (two hearths), and the 'high end' of the old hall house having a further two rooms (two hearths), making six hearths in all. Rex Lancefield, in his little book *Home in the North East Downs* (1987), uses the same hearth tax records to link owners with houses, although the list is considered by Lancefield as being 'mere speculation'. Despite these inevitable problems of linking owner with house, the hearth tax remains an interesting source of information about the local community.

Table 13: Hearth tax returns for Trimworth Borough, 1664.

Chargeable	Number of Hearths	House*
George Carter, gent.	8	Winchcombe
William Ruck	7	Ripple Farm
Geoffrey Graunt	9	?Tremworth
William Juce	6	?Crundale House
Stephen Gibbs	4	
Mr Allen, Clerke	4	Rectory
Thomas May	4	Glenwood Farm
William Chapman	3	Cakes Yoke
Stephen Lansfeild	3	Sole Street Farm
George Lansfeild	3	Simonwell Farm
Thomas Reynolds	1	
Stephen Quested	1	
Widdow Boulding	1	Little Ripple
William Smith exempt (because of poverty)		
Widdow Mason	1	
John Adman	1	
Thomas Rigden	1	
John Adley	1	
Nicholas Adman	1	
Edward Berch	1	Danewood
Edward Epps	1	
Thomas Baker	1	Thatch Cottage

* As identified by Rex Lancefield, *Home in the North East Downs*, 1987.

County record offices are a good source for records of hearth tax. For Kent there is a good set for 1664 at the Centre for Kentish Studies, but other years have not survived. The National Archives also have good records, and it is easy to check whether your parish or place is covered by doing an online search on: www.nationalarchives.gov. uk/e179. The number 'e179' refers to all medieval and early modern taxation records. A basic summary of hearth tax returns is provided by J. Gipson in *The Hearth Tax and other later Stuart tax lists and association rolls*, Federation of Family Historical Societies (1996).

WINDOW TAX

'The potential for window taxes for house history studies has so far been under utilised, probably because few knew what assessments existed.' (J. Gipson, M. Medleycott and D. Mills, *Land and Window Tax Assessments*, Federation of Family History Societies, 1993). The window tax was introduced in 1696 by the William and Mary Government to replace the earlier hearth tax, and was recast in new Acts in 1747 and 1797, before being repealed in 1851. The initial rate of tax was two shillings per house, except for those on poor relief. Houses with more than 10 windows paid eight shillings. The window tax was no more popular than the hearth tax. It was still felt to be an invasion, with the Crown being accused of taxing daylight itself, to the detriment of living conditions. It was certainly easier to calculate, because assessors did not require access to the house. Windows in certain service rooms, such as dairies, and shops attached to dwellings, were exempt, but rules were being constantly changed and evasion was rampant. Window openings could be blocked temporarily or permanently, often adversely affecting the symmetrical façades of houses. Camouflage was used, bribes were offered and the tax failed to raise the revenue it was seeking, which probably explains why the now familiar income tax was introduced in 1793.

The survival rate of the records is poor, and the best guide to availability is provided by the above reference, which lists the holdings of every county record office, county by county. The National Archives has a collection under series 'e182' but they are not well classified. Records for Canterbury parishes from 1752 to 1788 are at the Canterbury Cathedral Archives; other Kent parishes are at the Centre for Kentish Studies.

51 Ordnance Survey Extract, 1801 (revised to include railways in 1889), one inch to one mile.
This map represents the first area to be published in the one-inch series and shows the use of hachures to depict relief, but no field boundaries are shown.

CHAPTER 12

Maps, Plans and Surveys

Maps provide the visual record to supplement archival material, and are often good ways to begin research by locating the house within its administrative framework as well as its physical setting. A map is relatively easy to interpret and the researcher can build up a chronological picture of the growth and decline of settlement in the study area by studying a sequence of maps. Maps provide a record of building dates and subsequent changes in the layout of buildings, including extensions and demolition. Most people presented with a map of their home area will immediately and enthusiastically look for familiar landmarks. The map, therefore, represents a useful, varied and exciting source for researching the documentary history of a house. One must remember, however, that as with any historical document there are difficulties inherent in the use of old maps. They are often the result of the perceptions of one person who drew the map for a specific purpose. It is also important to know how accurate the map is in relation to, say, field shape and size. Maps may represent these features in a generalised way, while others have been drawn for the purpose of recording ownership and are therefore more likely to show accurate boundaries and areas. A comprehensive guide to their provenance, content, accuracy, location and uses is provided by Paul Hindle, *Maps for Local Historians* (Phillimore, 1998).

ORDNANCE SURVEY MAPS

In the 18th century, when Europe was in turmoil, there were real fears that the French Revolution might sweep across the Channel. The government responded by ordering its defence ministry, the Board of Ordnance, to begin a survey of Britain's southern coasts. The first 'one-inch' map of Kent was published in 1801, and within 20 years a third of England and Wales had been mapped at the one-inch scale (Fig. 49).

The demands of the Tithe Commutation Act, and the beginning of the railway era, both provided a need for more detailed maps at a larger scale, and in 1840 surveying began to produce the six-inch scale. Lancashire and Yorkshire were the first areas to be surveyed and published, giving us a valuable picture of two rapidly industrialising counties. The 25-inch scale was then adopted progressively from 1854 for the whole country, except for uncultivated areas which were only published at the six-inch scale. By 1888 the whole of England and Wales south of Yorkshire and Lancashire was surveyed. Both map scales have been revised at frequent intervals, changing to metric scales in 1969 (and causing problems of comparability for the local history researcher!). These earlier developments have been followed by new technologies culminating in the first computerised large-scale maps in 1973; the digital age had begun. The Ordnance Survey digitised the last of some 230,000 maps in 1995, making Britain the first country in the world to complete the programme of large-scale electronic mapping. The public still knows Ordnance Survey for its comprehensive range of printed leisure maps, yet electronic data now account for over 80 per cent of Ordnance Survey's turnover, underpinning a huge range of economic activity from crime fighting and conservation to marketing.

What is the relevance of the Ordnance Survey publications to the house researcher? The first edition of the one-inch maps, produced in 1801, does not show the detail required. Rural properties can often be identified but field boundaries are not shown. Roads and canals are more precisely indicated, and there is some attempt to show relief, firstly with hachures and then contours or hill shading. A few conventional signs are used for churches, woodlands and orchards, but there is no key. There is a good deal of archaeological information shown. Timeline Maps have produced facsimiles of the one-inch Old Series (1805 to 1874), designed to complement the current Landranger Series. Each Timeline map is produced to the same scale and covers the same area as the equivalent Landranger map. Used together, the past and the present come together in sharp focus. This is a fascinating series.

First editions of the six-inch maps (1:10,000 scale) and 25-inch maps (1:2,500 scale) are useful, and national surveys were carried out at these scales between 1853 and 1888. The 25-inch plans set new standards of accuracy. Fields and their boundaries are accurately represented, with each field or enclosure being numbered and acreages given (Fig. 50). Town plans were produced also at a much larger scale of 1:500 from 1850.

Contacts for the Ordnance Survey

Website: www.ordnancesurvey.co.uk – there is an 'historical mapping' homepage with details on ordering procedures.
Tel.: 08456 050505
Email: customerservices@ordnancesurvey.co.uk

Before purchasing, however, check the availability of historical O.S. maps in local libraries, archives, local councils, university libraries and geography departments. (Remember that O.S. maps over 50 years old can be freely copied, but the copying of anything more recent requires permission from the O.S.)

Another important source is the website 'A Vision of Britain Through Time' at www.visionofbritain.org.uk. This contains content on historical mapping. Information on local areas is obtained by entering postcodes or place-names, giving access to 19th- and 20th-century maps as well as census reports. Check also www.british-history.ac.uk, which is a digital library offering access to a wide range of primary source material. It offers access to two 19th-century Ordnance Survey map series in digital format; maps of the whole of Britain at 1:10,500 scale; and maps of major urban areas at 1:2,500 scale.

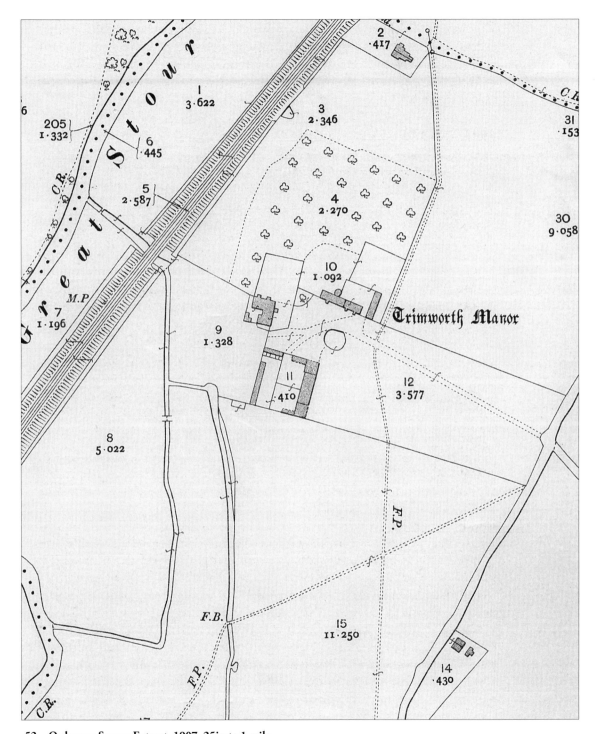

52   Ordnance Survey Extract, 1907, 25in to 1 mile.
Note the higher standards of accuracy, with fields and their boundaries clearly shown, and acreages given.

These sources will help to pinpoint your house at different periods and identify changes in your community and the landscape features of roads, railways, field boundaries, and growth or decline of the built environment. This can be illustrated by reference to the accompanying Ordnance Survey maps in which Trimworth Manor is located.

TITHE MAPS

Tithes were payments-in-kind of a tenth of the annual produce of land, payable to the parson of the parish. Although this practice had been in existence for centuries, the changing social and economic conditions of the 19th century made tithes both irrelevant and highly unpopular amongst rural landowners and village communities, especially as many growing urban and industrial areas escaped them. Under the Tithe Commutation Act of 1836, payments were to be commuted into fixed monetary payments, based on a seven-year average of the price of wheat, barley and oats taken across the country. A Tithe Commission helped to arbitrate disputed payments at the local level. Once agreed, the rent was apportioned among the landowners according to acreage and land quality. This clearly required detailed surveys of land ownership and land use, with accurate field measurements undertaken by local surveyors who worked under close instruction and supervision. About three-quarters of England and Wales was surveyed. Only a quarter of Northamptonshire has tithe maps, whereas Kent has virtually a complete tithe map coverage, usually at the scale of about twenty inches to the mile, providing a wonderful picture of the rural landscape in the 1840s.

Tithe maps and the house historian

Tithe maps show the footprint of each house and its associated farm buildings. In order to make full use of the maps, the researcher must consult the accompanying apportionment schedule. These large sheets give details of ownership, field names, state of cultivation or the actual crop planted, the acreage and the rent payable. Thus the agricultural economy of the parish can be reconstructed. Entries are arranged alphabetically by owners' names. Most maps will show enclosed fields by a solid line with each field given a number to coincide with field details in the apportionment book.

The tithe map relevant to Trimworth is of the parish of Crundale, surveyed in 1839 by Thomas Thurston of Ashford. Most of the farmland for Trimworth was in the ownership of Sir Edward Filmer, although the occupier is recorded as George Parkin. Land use included pasture, arable, hops and woodland. Water courses, roads, paths and buildings are clearly shown on the map, often differentiated by colour. Field names provide a useful source of information. Close to Trimworth is Kitchen Meadow, while adjoining the house is Moat Field. Little and Great Tithe fields are relevant to the purpose of the survey, while Strawberry Field, Oast Garden and Hop Garden Field suggest former land uses on land now recorded as arable or pasture. Extracts from the tithe map for Crundale are shown, together with a section of tithe apportionment for Crundale (Figs 51 and 52).

53 Tithe map extracts, 1839.
The footprint of each house and associated farm buildings is shown together with a wealth of landscape detail, beautifully differentiated in watercolours. Field numbers relate to the apportionment schedules (see Fig. 52). (Reproduced with permission of David White, Hunt Street Farm.)

54 Tithe Apportionment Schedule, 1839.
Numbers in the left margin refer to plot numbers on the tithe map. The apportionment schedules record field names, land use, acreage, and tithes due to the rector.

The apportionment is divided into columns listing the landowner, occupier, plot number, name and description of land and premises, state of cultivation, quantities in statute measures, names of tithe owners and other remarks. It is the first three columns that are of greatest interest to house historians, providing a link between properties and owners, and the census returns for that period.

The availability of tithe records

In general, three copies of each tithe map were made. The parish copy and diocesan copy are often found in county record offices, and this is the best place to begin a search. A third copy, and usually the best preserved, will be found in the National Archives in two series, IR30 for the maps, and IR29 for the apportionment schedules. Lists are arranged alphabetically by county, and thereafter by parish. Although in principle all copies are the same, in practice they may vary slightly in terms of amount of decoration and detail. The best source of information concerning availability of tithe maps is the publication by Kain and Oliver entitled *The Tithe Maps and Apportionments of England and Wales* (CUP, 1995). This lists the availability of all tithe maps by county and parish, together with information about date of survey, surveyor's name, features covered, etc. There is also an introduction for each county, giving useful information on accuracy. Background information on the tithe process is described in great detail in Kaine and Prince's publication *The Tithe Surveys of England and Wales* (CUP, 1985).

Finally it should be recognised that the tithe maps and awards represent one of the most complete records ever made of agriculture in England and Wales, and are a vital element in dating buildings and linking the buildings to owner occupiers and tenants.

ESTATE MAPS

Early surveys of estates were generally in written form, but increasingly landowners from the mid-16th century wanted cartographic surveys to accompany written documents. This was made possible by the development of surveying techniques, enabling landowners to appreciate the spatial arrangement of fields, boundaries and land-use acreages more clearly, as well as providing a document which had some legal basis. The best known of the early estate map-makers is Christopher Saxton, a professional land surveyor. Without commonly agreed map conventions, many landscape features are shown pictorially, such as 'sugarloaf hills'. Buildings are shown in side elevation, rather than plan view, and there is great elaboration on bigger buildings and churches. His maps, like those of other contemporary surveyors such as John Walker and John Norden, are functional and designed for a specific purpose.

During the 18th century, estate plans became better known and the features more accurately represented. There was a uniformity of style. The period 1700 to 1850 has been described by J.B. Harley in his book *Maps for Local Historians* (1972) as 'the golden age for the local land surveyor'. Their numbers declined as tithe maps and the

Ordnance Survey became more prominent, but we are fortunate that over 30,000 estate maps survive in a great variety of forms. The most likely place to find estate maps is the county record office. The Centre for Kentish Studies has an extremely useful publication, *Catalogue of Estate Maps 1590 to 1840*, published in 1973 and edited by F. Hull. The National Archives also have a collection, listed in map catalogues. However, many have not survived, or are in private hands, estate agencies or solicitors' offices. Another problem is that some maps find their way out of the county to which they refer. Nevertheless, they represent an invaluable snapshot for studying a single landowner's holding, which may cover a large part of one or more parishes, showing individual fields, boundaries, access, acreages and buildings. It should be remembered that the purpose of the map is usually to represent landownership, and for this reason the farmed landscape is usually more fully and accurately represented than settlements or buildings. Details of cultivation and land use are often given, and field names provide evidence of relict landscape features. Interpretation of some of these field names is assisted by publications of the English Place-Name Society, or *The Dictionary of Field Names*, published by J. Field in 1972. They often reveal just how many old features (ponds, streams, village sites, pits) have been lost with the intensification of agricultural practices.

The estate maps of Trimworth
1680 (U442AO)

In 1648, the Court Manor Rolls for Trimworth record the name of Sir Robert Filmer, who had married Dorothy Tuke in that year. Trimworth had become part of the Filmer Estate and remained so for over 260 years. In 1674 Sir Robert was created 1st Baronet, and when he died in 1674 the property was inherited by the 2nd Baronet, Sir Robert Filmer. Shortly afterwards, the estate map for Trimworth was drawn by Robert Spillett. The map, made in about 1680, is listed in the map collection of the Centre for Kentish Studies at Maidstone, but repeated requests over a period of two years failed to produce the map from the archives. Apparently it had been misfiled and finally came to light as a fragile parchment, impossible to unroll because it was so brittle. Eventually it was sent for conservation to Canterbury Cathedral Archives, where it was partly unrolled to reveal a water-damaged map over a metre long. Fortunately the best preserved section was around Trimworth Manor, gradually deteriorating towards the village of Crundale. A digital photograph was made, but the map is too fragile to be made available for public inspection and remains for the eyes of the archivists only. However, the digital photography is extremely clear and allows close inspection of the area around Trimworth. The whole map is reproduced here (Fig. 53) and the detail for Trimworth is shown in Fig 54.

Important features recorded are as follows:
- rivers, dykes and streams (the 'Grate' Stour)
- the names of landowners and tenants, together with names of owners and tenants for adjacent estates

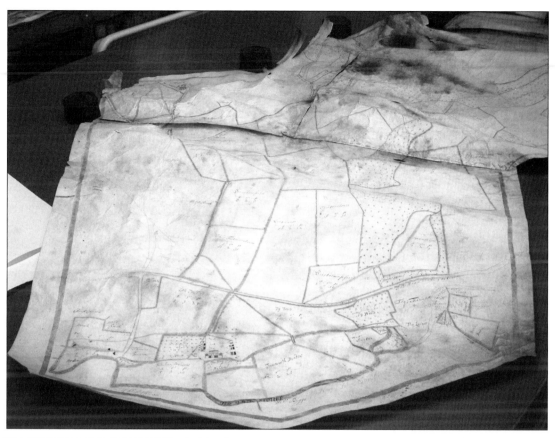

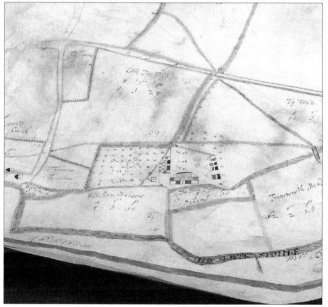

55 Estate map, Trimworth, 1680.
Produced shortly after Sir Robert Filmer inherited Trimworth, the map is nearly two metres long, water-damaged and very fragile. The best preserved section is around Trimworth, located towards the bottom edge of the map, deteriorating towards Crundale. (Reproduced with permission of Kent Archive service, and the Centre for Kentish Studies, U422 P10.)

56 Estate map, Trimworth, 1680, detail.
East is at the top of this map. To the north of the house is a building which may possibly be the chapel referred to in Domesday Monachorum and later documents. It is close to where the geophysical survey identified old building lines (see Fig. 17).

- field sizes in acres, rods and perches
- land use characteristics (woods are drawn with evenly spaced trees)
- field names such as Hog Field, Kitchen Meadow, etc.
- field boundaries drawn in colour, except when outside the ownership of the Filmer estate
- roads, footpaths and footbridges.

1720 (U2678)

In 1720, Sir Robert Filmer, the 2nd Baronet, died, and Trimworth was inherited by Sir Edward Filmer. The change of inheritance clearly required a new estate map which was drawn up 'from a scale of ten to a scale of twenty perch to the inch', by Henry Barforth from Staplehurst in about 1720. The area of the manor estate shown on this map is virtually identical to the area owned by his descendant, Sir Edward Filmer, over a hundred years later, and even bears a strong resemblance to the 1839 tithe map. However, despite this apparent continuity, the landscape details reveal a considerable amount of change, in terms of land use, field shape and size, extent of woodland, man-made drainage and trackways, and it is a fruitful exercise to monitor this change by comparing maps of different dates.

The 1720 map was rescued by the Dartford District Archaeological Group from the cellar of an estate agent who was disposing of stacks of old paper, sales documents and bags of maps. The map is more or less intact, but the parchment has become damaged in the north-east and north-west corners. Nevertheless it is a wonderful example of an 18th-century estate map and reveals a wealth of detail. A table in the margin of the map shows numbers of fields, field names, land use, and areal extent of fields. 'The last column of this table shews the letter and figure how to find any piece of land on this MAPP.'

There is a curtain cartouche around the title, which reads, 'a MAPP of the Manner of Tremworth being part of the estate of Sir Edwd. Filmer Bart.' The map border is decorated with compass rose and scale line, and there are wooden batons at the top and bottom. The most important details clearly concern the characteristics of the farmed landscape. Field boundaries are coloured. Those not maintained by the estate are shown with an indented line and ownership of adjoining lands is indicated (Esquire Thornell, Earl of Winchelsea, his lands; Mr Finch, etc.) Roads are named, foot paths and tracks indicated, and woods are shown as trees in side elevation. Houses are also shown in side elevation; the parsonage in Crundale is by far the biggest and most ornate, but sadly the building no longer exists. It is shown in an extract of the map reproduced in Fig. 55.

1861 (U1747P1)

Nearly 150 years later, in 1859, Sir Edmund Filmer, 9th Baronet, member of the Grenadier Guards and MP for West Kent from 1859 to 1865, inherited the Trimworth estate. Shortly after his inheritance, a fine bound volume of hand-drawn coloured maps showing all the 48 estates of Sir Edmund was produced. The maps, surveyed by George Ruck of Maidstone, demonstrate the enormous extent of Sir Edmund's

57   Estate map, Trimworth, 1720, detail.

On the death of Sir Robert Filmer, the house was inherited by Sir Edward Filmer who required the old estate map to be updated. This portion illustrates the cartographic style of the time, with the buildings of part of Crundale village shown in side elevation, rather than plan. (Reproduced with permission of the Kent Archive Service, and the Centre for Kentish Studies.)

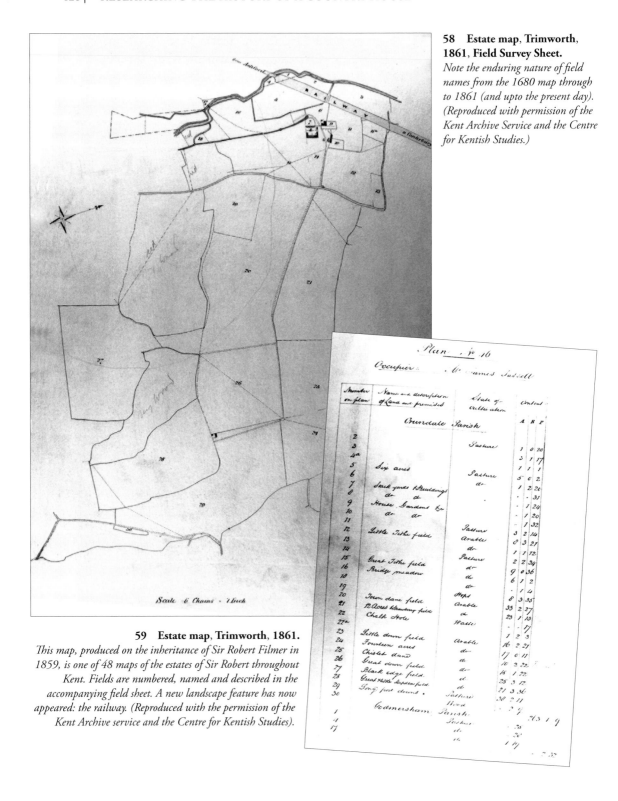

58 Estate map, Trimworth, 1861, Field Survey Sheet.
Note the enduring nature of field names from the 1680 map through to 1861 (and upto the present day). (Reproduced with permission of the Kent Archive Service and the Centre for Kentish Studies.)

59 Estate map, Trimworth, 1861.
This map, produced on the inheritance of Sir Robert Filmer in 1859, is one of 48 maps of the estates of Sir Robert throughout Kent. Fields are numbered, named and described in the accompanying field sheet. A new landscape feature has now appeared: the railway. (Reproduced with the permission of the Kent Archive service and the Centre for Kentish Studies).

estates throughout Kent, which included East Sutton, Sutton Valance, Ulcombe, Broomfield, Langley, Charing, Crundale (Trimworth), Chartham, Wye, Staplehurst, Headcorn, Marden, Lenham, Borden, Witchling, Ludham, Godmersham, Sevenoaks, Otford, Seal, Kemsing, Davington, Nonnington, and Boughton Monchelsea. All maps are drawn to the scale of six chains to one inch. The map of Trimworth (plan number 46) records a total acreage of 263 acres, one rod, nine perches, all farmed by the tenant, Mr James Tassell (Figs 56 and 57). As in the previous estate maps, the fields are numbered, named, and described in terms of land use, state of cultivation and areal extent. Field names are an enduring feature of the landscape, with many surviving unchanged from the 1680s map. However, a new feature has appeared on the map which was to have a huge impact on rural landscape change: the railway now cuts through the estate close to Trimworth Manor.

Maps and Plans for Public Schemes

Railway maps

Progressively, throughout the 19th century, railways replaced canals for the transport of heavy, bulky materials, with the period 1836/7 to 1846/7 seeing the most constructive activity. By 1848 there was a rail network of 4,600 miles, and the face of many local communities in rural and urban settings became irrevocably changed. For the local historian, deposited plans are a prime source of information. Plans were being drawn up for new route proposals which had to be deposited with the clerk of the peace and with Parliament. As well as indicating the route and major engineering impacts, they often show details of ownership, building and other local landscape features. Over one thousand such plans were lodged in 1844/5 alone.

Another useful map source is provided by indentures dealing with land sales between the landowner and the railway company. Such an indenture is available for Trimworth Manor where, in 1846, Sir Edward Filmer sold land to the South-Eastern Railway Company amounting to three roods, 31 perches. The indenture, and accompanying plan, deals with rights of drift-way and passage for Sir Edmund and his workers travelling on foot or horseback, and with cattle and other animals, with or without carts and carriages (Fig. 58).

The indenture notes that the company and its successors 'Shall and will at all times hereafter maintain and keep in good repair and condition, a substantial archway of nine foot headway at the least'. Land for sale is clearly designated in pink on the plan which is two and a half chains to the inch in scale. Of continuing significance to subsequent owners of Trimworth is the railway company agreement 'to construct and make for ever hereafter a water course or channel from and out of the Trimworth culvert into the River Stour, such water course or channel not to exceed sixteen foot in width at the water's edge, nor thirty foot at the surface of the soil'. This drainage channel remains a major part of the drainage network for the water meadows around Trimworth today.

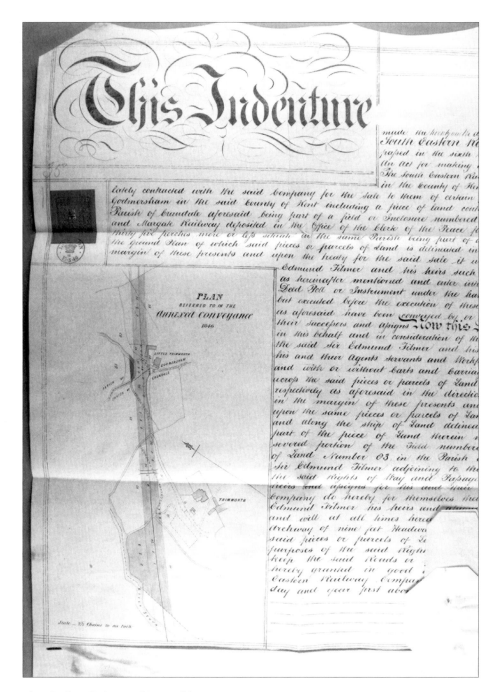

60 Railway Indenture Map, 1846.

This map deals with a land transfer between Sir Edward Filmer and South-Eastern Railway Company. The priority here is to identify the land under consideration for transfer, and required rights of way. (Reproduced with permission of the Kent Archive Service and the Centre for Kentish Studies U128 T4).

Maps of drainage and water management

Although not a primary source for the house historian, many rural properties have been featured in excellent drainage maps providing important information on techniques of land drainage, such as the complex networks of banks for water meadows. Despite changes in more recent agricultural practices, such systems have left physical traces on the landscape of the southern chalk lands, and are thus of archaeological and historical significance. Trimworth Manor is located in the Stour valley, and the water meadows adjacent to the river have been a valuable farming resource since the early settlement of the valley. Maps, accompanied by detailed documents, provide valuable information on the complex systems of channels, drains and dykes which have created efficient and profitable meadows. In addition, these sources provide further evidence of landownership, field shape and size, characteristics of agricultural practices, and location of built and natural landscape features.

In medieval times, the drainage and management of marshes, fens, and water meadows was often undertaken by representatives of the community, such as the 24 'sworn men' or 'jurats' responsible for maintaining the drainage features of Romney Marsh in the 13th century. Taxes were frequently levied on landowners for the upkeep and repair of banks, walls and dykes. These early management schemes led to a more organised system of control, frequently under the title of Commissions of Sewers. (The term 'sewer' before the mid-19th century included all flowing water channels, covered or uncovered, such as rivers and streams.) The first such commission was established in Lincolnshire in 1258 to maintain dykes, walls and bridges in Fenland and to preserve the low-lying land from flooding. The Bill of Sewers in 1531 regularised the formation of these commissions, and their numbers grew steadily (there were 49 such bodies still operating even as late as 1930).

Many local drainage matters continued to be influenced by the manorial courts in medieval and post-medieval times. These manorial courts, such as the one operating at Trimworth from 1648 to 1920, were an important element by which the principal local landowners could override any local opposition to drainage or irrigation schemes, and were probably strong enough to take on the commissions. It is quite likely that commissions included local landlords.

Trimworth and the Commission of Sewers Records

I am grateful to Joan Jeffery for her laborious efforts, working through officers' notebooks, accounts and minutes of the Commission for Trimworth/Tremworth. The inquisitions and presentments are huge legal documents of the Commission, and unlike many of the jury records are written by professional scribes and have often been checked very thoroughly. The Commission had been re-organised in the 1720s and new juries had been set up. These were required to survey a circuit of their territory and to present details of all properties to be taxed. The tax was known as a 'scot', and gave rise to the term 'scot free.' The River Stour from Ashford to Sturry

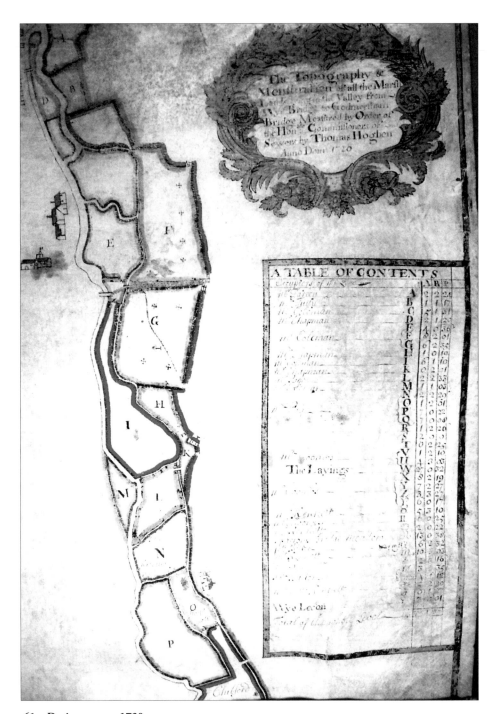

61   Drainage map, 1720.
'The Topography and Mensuration of all the Marshlands in the Stour Vallie from Wye Bridge to Godmersham Bridge. Measured by Order of the Hon. Commissioners of Sewers by Thomas Hogben.' A beautiful map full of information on the landscape. Trimworth is located towards the bottom of the map. (Reproduced with permission of the Kent Archive Service and the Centre for Kentish Studies, S/EK P76.)

has been divided into 'vallies', all numbered and listed, into which the circuits fitted. Every field, footpath, bridge and landowner was recorded.

The inquisition and presentment for the section of the Stour from Wye Bridge to Godmersham Bridge is dated 11 October 1740 (reference S/EKS1 Bundle 236-242), and covers an area of over one hundred acres. A short passage describing this circuit is reproduced below.

> N corner of Barn Field in Godmersham belonging to the said Sir Edward Filmer and from thence SW by a Hedge and Ditch at the NW side of Barn Field to the W corner thereof and from thence SW by a Pale Fence and a Hedge and Ditch on the SE side of a Little Meadow called the Hog Spott in Godmersham belonging to the said Sir Edward Filmer unto the S and W corner thereof leaving a messuage called Little Trimworth.

62   Cartouche from the drainage map, 1720.
Clearly an opportunity for the cartographer to indulge his creative talent. The large house to the right is Olantigh, in front of which the Stour divides to enclose Kitchen Meadow. (Reproduced with permission of the Kent Archive Service and the Centre for Kentish Studies, S/EK P76.)

The schedule also lists ownership and acreages so that charges can be made:

Owners	Occupiers/Tenants	a.	r.	p.
Sir Edward Filmer	Thos Page	6	3	23
"	Thos Page	6	1	39
"	Thos Page	6	0	8
"	Richard Smith	3	0	0
"	Geo Marsh	1	2	20
"	Geo Marsh	1	2	26
"	Geo Marsh	4	0	0

Research at the Centre for Kentish Studies was fortunate to reveal a wonderful map of the Stour Valley, drawn in 1720 by Thomas Hogben, which exactly coincides in area with the written document referred to above.

The map is in excellent condition, and is accompanied by a table, with letters corresponding to fields on the map, and recording occupiers and amount of land owned. The map measures one and a half metres in length with an elaborate coloured cartouche for title and scale, and shows the drainage details of the valley, including ditches and dykes, footpaths, bridges, field names and location of properties, drawn in side elevation (Figs 59 and 60).

NATIONAL LAND SURVEYS

At various times and for various reasons, governments have initiated national land surveys. In 1910 Lloyd George sought to raise revenues and re-adjust the burden of local taxation to make it more equitable by introducing a Finance Bill. Thirty years later, in an attempt to assist the war effort by increasing food productivity, the Ministry of Agriculture and Fisheries (MAF) surveyed all working farms to identify their productive state. For the house researcher and local historian, both of these surveys provide us with detailed information on land and property ownership, names of occupiers and owners, land use, land values, and other data which can be geographically referenced on accompanying large-scale maps. Both surveys will now be described and their importance illustrated with reference to Trimworth.

Lloyd George's 'Domesday' of landownership, 1910

By the end of the 19th century, the ownership of large sections of British countryside by relatively few people was seen to be a major cause of the poverty of the working people, which could be redressed only by taxing land values. The result was the Finance Bill of 1909, which required a valuation of all land to be carried out by the Inland Revenue, much to the disgust of the landowners. Not surprisingly, the House of Lords rejected the Bill, but after a year-long struggle and a General Election, the Finance Act was passed in 1910. The only precedent for this national assessment of land values was the Domesday Book itself, and thus the act became known as the 'New Domesday of Land'. The country was divided into valuation districts, each with a land valuation officer and a huge number of valuers who inspected properties and recorded data in field books, mapping the property boundary on Ordnance Survey maps at the largest available scale (usually 1:2,500).

There are three documents arising from this valuation.

Valuation books which summarise landownership and value under 40 columns, as follows:

Column Information

1	assessment number
2	poor rate number
3	name of occupier
4	name and address of owner
5	description of property
6	address of property
7	extent of holding
8	gross annual value of holding
9	rateable value
10	map reference
11 to 14	extent in acres, roods perches and yards
15 to 39	calculated figures for various valuations
40	observations and reference

Field Books, numbering about 95,000 and describing each property on four pages, including details of building materials, number of rooms, comments on repair and condition. Agricultural holdings included details of the state of cultivation, drainage, and land use.

Ordnance survey sheets, showing the boundaries of each assessment, together with identification number. Colour washes also identify the extent of ownership, and detached portions of land are braced together with red symbols.

These documents present enormous possibilities for the investigation of early 20th-century geography, society and economy, including land and property ownership, land occupation, building structures, housing, land use, the industrial and commercial structure of towns and cities, and the agricultural characteristics of rural Britain. For a more detailed analysis of this survey, see B. Short, *The Geography of England in 1910: an evaluation of Lloyd George's Domesday of Landowner-ship* (1989).

Trimworth and the New Domesday Survey

The starting point for this research was to obtain the 25-inch Ordnance Survey map of the area under consideration. The county record offices generally hold a less complete series of working maps than the National Archives, but it is always worth checking locally first. Fortunately, in this case, the county record office was able to provide the map showing the hereditaments, each numbered and colour-washed to identify extent of property (Fig. 61).

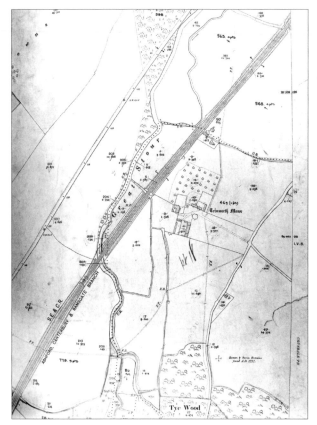

63 New Domesday Survey, 1910.
This map shows the hereditaments (numbers allocated for the purpose of land valuation), each colour-washed to identify extent of the property. (Trimworth is number 469.)

The hereditament number made it possible to retrieve the valuation book identifying all individual properties within the parish (Fig. 62). Trimworth is shown to be occupied by Walter Gibbons and the owner recorded as Sir Robert Marcus Filmer, who at the time also owned Denwood Farm in Crundale. The farm was over 326 acres, of which 256 acres was farmland. Gross value of the land and buildings was £5,108, and the value of agricultural land for agricultural purposes was £3,474. Although useful, most of the information is limited to land evaluation for purposes of taxation. Of more direct interest to the house historian is the field book, containing a fuller description of the farm characteristics. This was not available at the county record office, so the search was widened to the National Archives, using the class IR58. This allowed the valuation district to be identified, from which it was possible to find the field book containing four pages of description for Trimworth (IR5830792), (Fig. 63). Walter Gibbons had been tenant since 1904, paying an annual rental of £200 in addition to rates and taxes. He was also responsible for cost of repairs to the interior plus one third of the labour cost of these repairs. Trimworth Manor Farm is described as follows:

> brick and tile built house containing seven bedrooms, dining and drawing rooms, kitchen, scullery, dairy and garden. Pair of brick and tile-built cottages each containing two bedrooms and two down. Brick and slate built cottage containing three up and three down, ditto containing four up and three down. The buildings comprises of brick, timber, and tile oast house, coach house, storeroom, three loose boxes, and chaff bin; loft over and stabling for four.

Other buildings on the site included wagon lodges, implement sheds, chaff stores, cow houses and pigsties. The farm had an income of £326 from sporting activities and £120 from the sale of timber.

64 New Domesday Survey, 1910, **valuation book for Crundale parish.**
Trimworth (469) is listed fourth, a farm of 256 acres with a value for agriculture of £3,474.

The National Farm Survey, 1941 to 1943

In 1940, the Ministry of Agriculture, Fisheries and Food, conscious of the need for increased productivity to feed the country during time of war, conducted a comprehensive survey of 300,000 farms and small-holdings in England and Wales. Farm plans were produced identifying boundaries and fields. Written returns were made giving a full picture of the state of the farm, its fertility, equipment and general management. For the house historian researching a rural property, this is a very good source, and it can also be valuable in monitoring landscape change in a suburban location where farmland has been lost to the built environment. This loss of agricultural land was particularly significant in the inter-war period and following the Second World War, when housing was being built at lower densities on green-field sites.

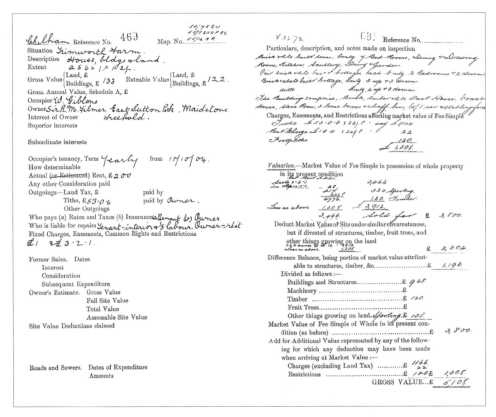

65 New Domesday Survey, 1910, Field Book (part entry for Trimworth).
This book contains a fuller description of farm properties and buildings, with details of the evaluation.

Trimworth and the Farm Survey, 1941 to 1943

No records were available at the county record office, but a visit to the National Archives was more successful. The maps are in series MAFF 73, and arranged alphabetically by county. Each county sheet is divided into numbered grids, allowing individual properties to be identified. Trimworth was colour-washed with reference number, and to obtain the record sheets, series MAFF 32 was used to identify the relevant parish. The researcher is provided with a brown envelope containing the record sheets for all farms in the parish (Fig. 64).

The records reveal that Trimworth Manor was now in the ownership of J.H. Louden of Olantigh Wye. The farm was being run by Edward Hardy, with Mr J. Hodgson as the tenant. It was a medium-sized mixed farm, producing wheat, barley, oats and clover together with pasture and rough grazing. Small amounts of kale, rape and mustard were also grown. Livestock included 37 cattle, 240 sheep and lambs, 12 pigs, and 70 poultry. The record sheets indicate a high proportion of land described as 'light' but the overall condition of the arable land and pasture is described as 'poor,' with heavy infestations of couch, dock and charlock. The summary comment on the

MINISTRY OF AGRICULTURE AND FISHERIES.
THE DEFENCE REGULATIONS, 1939, AND THE AGRICULTURAL RETURNS ORDER, 1939.
RETURN WITH RESPECT TO AGRICULTURAL LAND ON 4th JUNE, 1941.

	CROPS AND GRASS	Statute Acres		LIVE STOCK on holding, on 4th June, including any sent for sale on that or previous day			Number (in figures)
1	Wheat	20	43	Cows and Heifers in milk			2
2	Barley	23	44	Cows in Calf, but not in milk			
3	Oats	31	45	Heifers in Calf, with first Calf			4
4	Mixed Corn with Wheat in mixture		46	Bulls being used for service			1
5	Mixed Corn without Wheat in mixture		47	Bulls (including Bull Calves) being reared for service			
6	Rye		48	OTHER CATTLE	2 years old and above	Male	
7	Beans, winter or spring, for stock feeding		49			Female	11
8	Peas, for stock feeding, not for human consumption		50		1 year old and under 2	Male	4
9	Potatoes, first earlies		51			Female	8
10	Potatoes, main crop and second earlies		52		Under 1 year old:— (a) For rearing (excluding Bull Calves being reared for service)		7
11	Turnips and Swedes, for fodder		53		(b) Intended for slaughter as Calves		
12	Mangolds		54	TOTAL CATTLE and CALVES			37
13	Sugar Beet		55	Steers and Heifers over 1 year old being fattened for slaughter before 30th November, 1941			5
14	Kale, for fodder	14	56	SHEEP OVER 1 YEAR OLD	Ewes kept for further breeding (excluding two-tooth Ewes)		110
15	Rape (or Cole)	11	57		Rams kept for service		3
16	Cabbage, Savoys, and Kohl Rabi, for fodder		58		Two-tooth Ewes (Shearing Ewes or Gimmers) to be put to the ram in 1941		
17	Vetches or Tares		59		Other Sheep over 1 year old		26
18	Lucerne		60	SHEEP UNDER 1 YEAR OLD	Ewe Lambs to be put to the ram in 1941		
19	Mustard, for seed		61		Ram Lambs for service in 1941		
20	Mustard, for fodder or ploughing in	4	62		Other Sheep and Lambs under 1 year old		101
21	Flax, for fibre or linseed		63	TOTAL SHEEP and LAMBS			240
22	Hops, Statute Acres, not Hop Acres		64	Sows in Pig			4
23	Orchards, with crops, fallow, or grass below the trees		65	Gilts in Pig			
24	Orchards, with small fruit below the trees		66	Other Sows kept for breeding			
25	Small Fruit, not under orchard trees		67	Barren Sows for fattening			
26	Vegetables for human consumption (excluding Potatoes), Flowers and Crops under Glass		68	Boars being used for service			
27	All Other Crops not specified elsewhere on this return or grown on patches of less than ¼ acre		69	ALL OTHER PIGS (not entered above)	Over 5 months old		
28	Bare Fallow		70		2—5 months		8
29	Clover, Sainfoin, and Temporary Grasses for Mowing this season	24	71		Under 2 months		
30	Clover, Sainfoin, and Temporary Grasses for Grazing (not for Mowing this season)		72	TOTAL PIGS			12
31	Permanent Grass for Mowing this season		73	POULTRY If none, write "None"	Fowls over 6 months old		70
32	Permanent Grass for Grazing (not for Mowing this season), but excluding rough grazings	84	74		Fowls under 6 months old		
33	TOTAL OF ABOVE ITEMS, 1 to 32 (Total acreage of Crops and Grass, excluding Rough Grazings)	207	75		Ducks of all ages		
			76		Geese of all ages		
34	Rough Grazings—Mountain, Heath, Moor, or Down Land, or other rough land used for grazing on which the occupier has the sole grazing rights	40	77		Turkeys over 6 months old		
			78		Turkeys under 6 months old		
			79	TOTAL POULTRY			70

LABOUR actually employed on holding on **4th June.** The occupier, his wife, or domestic servants should not be entered.

			Number (in figures)
35	WHOLETIME REGULAR WORKERS	Males, 21 years old and over	1
36		Males, 18 to 21 years old	1
37	If none, write "None"	Males, under 18 years old	
38		Women and Girls	
39	CASUAL (SEASONAL or PART-TIME) WORKERS	Males, 21 years old and over	
40		Males, under 21 years old	
41		Women and Girls	1
42	TOTAL WORKERS		3

Form No. C 47/S.S.Y.   M.14060. 4/41. (52-2551)

80	GOATS OF ALL AGES			

	HORSES on holding on 4th June			Number (in figures)
81	Horses used for Agricultural Purposes (including Mares kept for breeding) or by Market Gardeners	(a) mares		2
82		(b) geldings		
83	Unbroken Horses of 1 year old and above	(a) mares		
84		(b) geldings		
85	Light Horses under 1 year old			
86	Heavy Horses under 1 year old			
87	Stallions being used for service in 1941			
88	All Other Horses (not entered above)			
89	TOTAL HORSES			2

66 National Farm Survey, 1941.

This is the entry for Trimworth, showing details of the farm economy (land use and livestock).

farm as a whole reads, 'this farm was taken over by Mr Hardy last Michaelmas. All ploughing and winter cropping has been done. Although the farm is not yet clean it must be considered an "A" Class farm.'

This discussion of National Farm Surveys has dwelt heavily on surveys of particular relevance to rural locations, providing excellent insights into land ownership, tenancy, farm techniques and management. Candid notes on the quality of the farm and competence of the farmer are revealing. This is all good information, indicating how people lived. At Trimworth in 1940 water supply was from a well and run off from the roof, and there was no electricity supply. The surveys also provide excellent continuity in monitoring building and landscape change, from estate maps and tithe maps through into the 20th century. From a personal point of view, the surveys introduced me to using the National Archives for the first time. Initially this can be a daunting experience, but the published finding aids, as well as the expertise, professionalism and welcoming nature of enquiry desk staff makes the experience a rewarding one.

County Maps

The value of county maps to the house historian lies in their ability to create an interesting, generalised picture of the environment in which buildings are set. Their limitation, however, can be the varying standards of accuracy, particularly since they were superseded by the Ordnance Survey maps with their superior, consistent standard of survey and mapping.

The first complete set of county maps was surveyed and produced by Christopher Saxton in the middle of the 16th century, followed by the other great Elizabethan cartographers, John Norden and William Smith. Their work was extensively copied and redesigned by Camden in his *Britannia* of 1607, and by John Speed in 1610, whose recognition of using other sources was expressed in the phrase 'I have put my sickle into other men's corne'. Apart from further plagiarism and reprinting, little progress was made until the 17th century. Then the incentive of grants to cartographers from the Society of Arts in 1759, as well as local demand, resulted in a great surge of county and local maps.

Content often depended on the background of the cartographer, but all were able to provide details of the landscape, showing land use, industrial sites, communications and towns. They were generally based on fairly accurate triangulation rather than field sketches, and provide us with a series of maps, which, followed by the Ordnance Survey production, give us a continuing record of change in the landscape over 200 years. The value of the county map to the house historian will now be illustrated with reference to Kent, and the coverage provided by Andrews, Dury and Herbert in 1769, and Edward Hasted in 1797.

Andrews, Dury and Herbert, 1769

This collection of 25 sheets with a key sheet, covering the county, was published by Act of Parliament in 1769, and provides a valuable map resource at the scale of two inches to one mile. The original sheets have been reproduced in book form by Harry Margary of Lympne Castle in 1968, who specialised in high-quality facsimiles of rare 16th- to 19th-century maps. The title page of the collection describes the maps as containing 'roads, lanes, churches, towns, villages, noblemen and gentlemen's seats, roman roads, hills, rivers, woods, cottages and everything remarkable in the County, together with the division of lathes and their subdivision into hundreds'. Map 14 in the collection features the Hundred of Felborough in which Trimworth is located (Fig. 65).

Names of some properties and property owners are shown and there is an attractive, but not particularly accurate, representation of relief, by the use of hachures and shading. There are no field boundaries, and the interpretation of land use is limited to the extent of woodland. However, the maps do allow some analysis of continuity and change in the built environment of towns, villages and roads, as well as in place-names.

Hasted, 1797

In Chapter 2, the written descriptions by Hasted relating to Trimworth were examined, but this section is about maps and their relevance to an interpretation of local history and the geography of the time. One can judge the enormity of the task undertaken by Hasted in compiling maps of the 66 hundreds in the county at the scale of two inches to one mile. Everitt regards the maps as being 'an immense improvement on anything that had gone before indeed in most cases there was nothing earlier and in consequence they are of much topographical interest'. Everitt had obviously overlooked the Andrews, Dury and Herbert coverage completed nearly thirty years earlier, and at the same scale. Undoubtedly, Hasted was aware of these earlier maps, because he relied heavily on sources from the Canterbury Cathedral library, in which was deposited the 1769 maps. (A piece of the Dury Atlas was found among Hasted's papers). 'Take any of Hasted's maps and compare them with the corresponding section of the Andrews and Dury Atlas, and their source is at once apparent.' Apparent, too, is the relevance of Boteler's observation that Andrews and Dury 'made a shocking work of their survey of East-Kent'. The source of this quote is from Boyle in his publication *In Quest of Hasted*, published in 1984 by Phillimore (see p.45).

Whatever the source of Hasted's maps, and although they are not characterised by perfect accuracy or artistic beauty, they do represent an enormous undertaking to represent the landscape diversity of Kent. Unfortunately, they do not represent an advance on the 1769 map in terms of detail or accuracy. An extract of the Felborough Hundred containing Trimworth is reproduced here, and can be directly compared with the earlier maps of Andrews, Dury and Herbert (Fig. 66).

Sales Catalogues

When a large property was being sold, the owner usually enlisted the help of an estate agent, solicitor or auctioneer who compiled a catalogue to provide information for

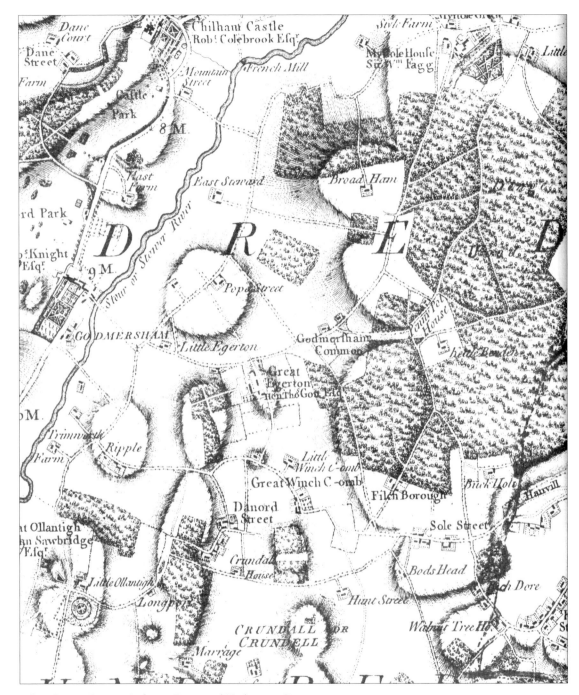

67   County Survey, Andrews, Drury and Herbert, 1769.
There are no field boundaries shown and land use is restricted to woodland, but the maps allow some analysis of continuity and change in the landscape when compared with earlier estate maps and later O.S. maps. This map is part of the hundred of Felborough in which Trimworth is located. The original map scale was two inches to one mile.

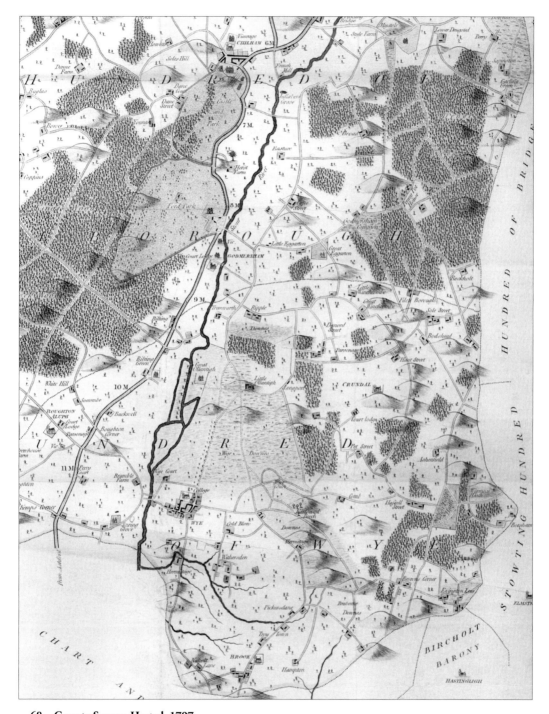

68   County Survey, Hasted, 1797.

This extract of the Hundred of Felborough covers a similar area to Fig. 65 and allows a comparison of style and detail. The original map scale was two inches to one mile.

69   Sales Catalogue, Trimworth, 1920.
The historical link with Odo, half brother of William the Conqueror, is used as a selling point, as well as the 'excellent sporting' offered within the estate. Many of the buildings listed remain, most having now been converted to residential use.

LOT 9

(Coloured Pink on Plan)

A RESIDENTIAL, AGRICULTURAL AND SPORTING PROPERTY

The Old Manor House of Trimworth

together with Land, Buildings, four Cottages, and 40 acres of Sporting Woodlands, in all

301A.   0R.   25P.

Pleasantly situated in the Stour Valley to the North of Olantigh Park, and within a mile of Godmersham Village.

Odo of Baieux, half brother of William the Conqueror, had an estate at Trimworth.

EXCELLENT SPORTING

particularly the partridge shooting, which is considered to be among the finest in the locality.

THE HOUSE

built in the style of the Jacobean period, is of brick, timber-framing and plaster, with tiled roof. The quaint Porch, with its carved barge boards and leaded windows, is of great interest to the antiquarian. The accommodation comprises :

GROUND FLOOR : Porch, Hall, Dining Room, Drawing Room, Kitchen, Dairy, Scullery, Larder, Pantry, also other Larders which might be adapted as extra reception rooms by a small outlay.

FIRST FLOOR : Six Bedrooms, Nursery, Bathroom, W.C.

NOTE.—The Bathroom Fittings are the property of the tenant.

FOUR SEMI-DETACHED COTTAGES

brick-built with tiled or slated roofs, and each containing Lobby, Sitting Room, Kitchen, Scullery, and two Bedrooms. Pump and Well Water. Large Gardens.

THE FARM BUILDINGS

which enclose a picturesque green, are all built of brick with tiled and slated roofs, and include range of three Loose Boxes, Saddle Room, Corn House, Trap House, a four-stall Stable and Chaff Bin, two Loose Boxes, Men's Bothy over, Oast, Granaries over, two Cowhouses for six and five respectively, with Root House and Feeding Passage, a three-bay Waggon Lodge, Barn, another Waggon Lodge, Granary, two open Bullock Lodges and Yard, range of five Fatting Lodges, Root House, five Piggeries.

In Field No. 95 there is a timber and iron Building consisting of Loose Box, a four-bay open Cattle Lodge and Yard.

Lot Seventeen.

(Coloured Pink on Plan D.)

The Valuable Freehold Property,

HAVING AN AREA OF ABOUT

301 acres   2 roods   8 poles,

In the PARISHES OF CRUNDALE AND GODMERSHAM,

KNOWN AS

TRIMWORTH MANOR FARM,

COMPRISING :

AN OLD MANOR HOUSE,

Built of Brick, part Plaster, half Timber and Tile Hung, with Tiled Roof and

Curious Old Carved Porch,

AND CONTAINING :

Eight Bedrooms, Dressing Room, Closet and Linen Cupboard, Front and Back Staircases, Paved Hall, Two Reception Rooms, Store Room (paved), Kitchen, Larder, Dairy, Pantry and Scullery; Brick and Tiled Coal-house and Room over; Garden.

A Range of Brick, Timber and Tiled Buildings,

comprising: Coach-house, Store, Rider's Stable of Three Stalls, Harness Room, with Granary over all; Oast with one round Kiln.

A BRICK AND TILED STABLE,

with Two Loose Boxes and Stalls for Four Horses.

A BLOCK OF FARM BUILDINGS,

comprising : Timber and Slated Barn, Granary, Waggon Lodge, Two Open Bullock Lodges, Cart Lodge, Meal House; a range of Timber and Tiled Bullock and Cow Lodges; Pigsties.

There is also a Bullock Lodge on the Downs.

Near the Homestead is

A PAIR OF BRICK AND SLATED COTTAGES,

Each containing Three Bedrooms, Parlour, Kitchen and Scullery, Closet and Wood Lodge (one Cottage has a Mate's Room in addition).

25   *[continued overleaf.*

---

70   Sales Catalogue, Trimworth, 1911.
The catalogue includes details of land use for each plot within the 253 acres of farmland.

potential purchasers. The format of these documents varies, but for larger properties with land they are usually accompanied by a map and lists of the main buildings and outhouses, with details of building materials, number and use of rooms. The best source of these sales records is usually the county record office, often catalogued under property name. The National Archives also hold a collection of catalogues, dating from the 19th century. The documents are arranged by county, and thereafter the name of the place that is listed in the Sales Catalogue.

Sales catalogues for Trimworth Manor

In 1911, the estates of Sir Robert Marcus Filmer were auctioned in the City of London. One of the lots in the estate was Trimworth Manor Farm, which had an area of over 301 acres and was let to Mr Walter Gibbons on a yearly Michaelmas tenancy for a rent of £200 ('Tenant does all internal repairs, and for other repairs the Landlord funds material and half labour'). The catalogue also gives details of the land use for each plot, and these are located on a plan. The farmed landscape consisted of over 253 acres (Fig. 67).

In 1920, the property was again offered for sale as a residential, agricultural and sporting property (Fig. 68). Its historical significance was clearly considered to be a selling point because the property notice refers to Odo of Baieux, half-brother of William the Conqueror, as a notable resident. The description of the farm buildings suggested this was a flourishing mixed farm enterprise for sheep, cattle, pigs, arable and pasture with 40 acres of sporting woodland. Of great interest is the photograph of Trimworth Manor and farm buildings (Fig. 69).

71   Trimworth Manor, from the 1920 Sales Catalogue.

Conclusions

The Ordnance Survey is usually a good starting point for researching the history of a house, providing an indication of the dates of construction and locating the building within its administrative and geographical setting. It allows the researcher to gain familiarity with the location. Research can usually be undertaken locally, widening the search as more specific maps are required. This section is not a comprehensive survey of map sources. Social maps which depict health, economic and social status of inhabitants at various times in the past have not been illustrated. Mortality maps of the flu and cholera epidemics in the 19th century raise interesting questions of environmental influences on patterns of disease (epidemiology). The distribution of poverty, crime and changing patterns of ethnicity all reveal interesting patterns and relationships of great significance to the lives of people in different localities, particularly urban. Finally, it is important to reiterate a point made earlier that there are inherent dangers in the use of maps as evidence. One needs to be aware of the main purpose for which the map was made and to consider its accuracy in relation to features of secondary importance to the map maker. The map cannot show every landscape detail because of the constraints of scale and the selectivity of the map maker, and therefore absence of evidence is not necessarily evidence that the features does not exist.

72 Trimworth Manor as it is today.

References & Further Reading

General Texts and Guides on House History

Adolph, A., *Tracing Your Home's History* (Collins, 2006)

Alcock, N.W., *Documenting the History of Houses* (British Records Association, 2003)

Austin, M. *et al.*, *Be Your Own House Dectective* (BBC Books, 1997)

Barratt, N., *House History Starter Pack* (Public Records Office, 2002)

Barratt, N., *Tracing the History of Your House*, 2nd edn (National Archives, 2006)

Beech, G. and Mitchell, R., *Maps for Family and Local History* (National Archives Publications, 2004)

Breckon, B. and Parker, J., *Tracing the History of Houses* (Countryside Books, 1995)

Brooks, P., *How to Research your House: Every Home Tells a Story* (How To Books Ltd, 2007)

Jenkins, S., *England's Thousand Best Houses* (Penguin/Allen Lane, 2003)

Style, C., *House Histories for Beginners* (Phillimore, 2006)

Iredale, D. and Barrett, J., *Discovering Your Old House* (Shire Publications, 2002)

Useful Website

www.nationalarchives.gov.uk/catalogue/researchguidesindex.asp

(This is an index of all the Research Guides published by the National Archives and is an invaluable source for many aspects of house and family history research.)

Chapter 1: Getting Started

Buck, W.S.B., *Examples of Handwriting 1550-1650* (Society of Geneologists, 1996)

Chapman, C., *How Heavy, How Much and How Long? Weights, Money and Other Measures Used by Our Ancestors* (Lochin, 1995)

Marshall, H., *Palaeography for Family and Local Historians* (Phillimore, 2004)

Myerson, J., *Home: the Story of Everyone who Ever Lived in Your House* (Harper Perennial, 2005)

Stephens, W.B. *Sources for English Local History* (Phillimore, 1994)

Stuart, D., *Latin for Local and County Historians: a beginners guide* (Philimore, 1995)

Useful Websites

www.a2a.org.uk

(An ongoing search facility of collections held in archives in England and Wales.)

www.british-history.ac.uk

(A digital library of local source materials including O.S. maps.)

www.herehistory.kent.org.uk

(Wide range of source materials research on house history or family history.)

www.hiddenhousehistory.co.uk
  (Illustrative examples of case studies of house history.)
www.oralhistory.org.uk/advice
  (Advice on how to run your own oral history project.)
www.nationalarchives.gov.uk/archon
  (Gives contact details for archives, libraries and museums in the UK.)
www.visionofbritain.org.uk
  (Enables place-name or post-code searches of socio-economic data for local
  communities.)

Chapter 2: Historical Descriptions and Travels

The easiest way to consult histories and travels of your local environment is through a number
  of excellent websites.
www.british-history.ac.uk
  (Contains digitised county histories, such as Samuel Lewis, *Topographic Dictionary
  of England*, 1848.)
www.englandspastforeveryone.org.uk
  (A series of county projects bringing together authors, researchers and local people in
  an interactive website.)
www.localhistories.org
  (Contains online histories of many parishes.)
www.victoriacountyhistory.ac.uk
  (Described as 'the greatest publishing project in English local history'.)
www.visionofbritain.org.uk
  (This has digitised versions of travels such as Cobbett's *Rural Rides* with place-names
  highlighted and links to other sources.)

Chapter 3: The Landscape as a Document

Aston, M., *Interpreting the Landscape: Landscape, Archaeology and Local History* (Routledge,
  1985)
Hoskins, W.G., *The Making of the English Landscape* (Hodder & Stoughton, 2005)
Muir, R., *The New Reading of the Landscape: Fieldwork in Landscape History* (University of
  Exeter Press, 2000)
Rackham, O., *The History of the Countryside* (Phoenix, Orion Publishing, 2000)
Rippon, S., *Historic Landscape Analysis: deciphering the countryside* (Council for British
  Archaeology, 2004)
Short, B., *England's Landscape: the South East* (Collins, for English Heritage, 2006)

Useful Websites
www.bgs.ac.uk
  (Allows you to check details of geology and fossil localities, site investigations and
  map extracts.)
www.digital-documents.co.uk
  (Gives details of 85,000 archaeological sites with free searches for limited results.)
www.english-heritage.org.uk
  (Details of the Public Archive (National Monuments Record) including online resources,

photo collections and local studies resource packs of your local area containing aerial photographs, listed buildings in the parish and an archaeological database.)

www.environmentagency.gov.uk/maps

(Allows a place-name or postcode search to discover 'What's in Your Backyard?')

www.ordnance.co.uk

(The Ordnance Survey website for details of all products and prices.)

www.pastscape.org

(The English Heritage website, which is a quick and easy way to search nearly 400,000 records with links to maps, aerial photographs and other websites.)

CHAPTER 4: THE HOUSE AS A DOCUMENT

Alcock, N.W. *et al.*, *Recording Timber-Framed Buildings: an illustrated glossary* (Council for British Archaeology, 1996)

Barnwell, P.S. and Adams, A.T., *The House Within: interpreting medieval houses in Kent* (HMSO, 1994)

Breckon, B. *et al.*, *Tracing the History of Houses* (Countryside Books, 2003)

Clifton-Taylor, A., *The Pattern of English Building* (Faber, 1987)

Cunnington, P., *How Old is Your House?* (Marston House, 1999)

Mercer, E., *English Vernacular Houses* (HMSO, 1995)

Pragnell, H., *Britain: a guide to architectural styles from 1066 to the present day* (Batsford, 2002)

Warren, J. (ed.), *Wealden Buildings: studies in Kent, Sussex and Surrey* (Coach Publishing, 1990)

Yorke, T., *The Country House Explained* (Countryside Books, 2003)

Useful Websites

www.bricksandbrass.co.uk

(Illustrates the way social change has influenced building style.)

www.buildinghistory.org

(For sources on building history with good references to online and printed sources, regularly updated.)

www.imagesofengland.org.uk

(All listed buildings are featured with details of construction, including photographs.)

www.lookingatbuildings.org.uk

(Contains a useful glossary of architectural terms, building types, architectural styles, building materials and methods of construction.)

www.spab.org.uk

(The website of the Society for the Protection of Ancient Buildings, with a good deal of technical information.)

CHAPTER 5: EARLY WRITTEN RECORDS

Place-Names

Gelling, M., *Place-names in the Landscape* (Dent, 1984)

Gelling, M., *Signposts to the Past* (Phillimore, 2010)

Glover, J., *Place-Names of Kent* (Batsford, 1970)

Mills, A.D., *A Dictionary of British Place-names* (Oxford Paperback, 2003)

Wallemberg, J.K., *Place-names of Kent* (Lundequistska Bokhandein, 1934)

Whynne-Hammond, C., *English Place-names Explained* (Countryside Books, 2005)

Useful Websites

www.gazetteer.co.uk
> (Lists over 500,000 place-names along with their grid reference.)

www.nottingham.ac.uk/english/ins/kepn/search.php
> (A digital map-based guide to the linguistic origins of England's town and village names.)

Anglo-Saxon Charters

Sanders, W.B., *Facsimiles of Anglo-Saxon Manuscripts*, 3 vols (1878-84). Available at the British Library.

Sawyer, P.H., *Anglo-Saxon Charters: an annotated list and bibliography* (Royal Historical Society, 1968)

Useful Website

www.trin.cam.ac.uk/chartwww/
> (The website of the British Academy and Royal Historical Society on Anglo-Saxon Charters, maintained by Trinity College Cambridge.)

www.aschart.kcl.ac.uk
> (Access to web-based information about Anglo-Saxon charters.)

Domesday Book

Darby, H.C., *The Domesday Geography of South-East England* (Cambridge, 1962)
> This is a classic, containing a detailed chapter for Kent by Isla Campbell.

Williams, A. and Marton, G.H. (eds), *Domesday Book: a Complete Translation* (Penguin Classics, 2003). This is an unabridged translation into English with an index of places and a glossary of terms.

Useful Websites

www.domesdaybook.co.uk
> (Plenty of background on the compilation and contents, with information on life of the time, landowners etc., together with a search facility.)

www.medievalgeneology.org.uk
> (Focuses on Domesday for the genealogist; worth using for other medieval sources such as deeds, wills, manorial records.)

www.nationalarchives.gov.uk/domesday
> (An excellent site with copious background information and an easy-to-use search facility for text and images.)

Domesday Monachorum

Douglas, D.C., *Domesday Monachorum* (Royal Historical Society, 1944). Available at Canterbury Cathedral Archives and Centre for Kentish Studies.

Everitt, A., *Continuity and Colonisation: the evolution of Kentish settlement* (Leicester University Press, 1986) Contains a series of maps showing geographical dispersal of churches in Kent and the evolution of Minster lands.

Ward, G., 'The list of Saxon churches in the Domesday Monachorum', *Archeologia Cantiana*, vol.45 (1933), pp.60-89. This article also explains the hierarchy of the churches in Kent.

Useful Website

www.kentarcheology.org.uk

> (Click Research, go to Victoria County History, and see the text of the D.M. together with an index of personal and place-names mentioned in the text.)

CHAPTER 6: EARLY HOUSE OCCUPANCY

Inquisition Post-Mortem (IPM)

The IPM is regarded as among the most genealogist-friendly records and is the mainstay of traditional medieval geneology, although some of the records are in Latin. Records are available at the National Archives, and it is likely that most county libraries and archives will have printed versions of these records. The National Archives have published a user leaflet on the IPM which is also available online.

See also: West, J., *Village Records,* 2nd edn (Chichester, 1982), Ch. 2

Parish Registers

Humphery-Smith, C., *The Phillimore Atlas and Index of Parish Registers* (Phillimore, 2003)

Tate, W., *The Parish Chest* (Cambridge University Press, 1969)

Useful Website

www.familysearch.org

> (Allows a comprehensive search of family tree and geneology records.)

CHAPTER 8: LATER HOUSE OCCUPANCY

Census Returns

Annal, D., *Using Census Returns, pocket guides to family history* (Public Records Office, 2002).

Chapman, C., *Pre-1841 Census and Population Listings in the British Isles* (Geneological Publishing Company, 1996)

Higgs, E., *Making Sense of the Census Revisited: census records for England and Wales, 1801-1901* (HMSO London, 2005)

Lumas, S., *Making Use of the Census*, 4th edn (Public Records Office, 2002)

National Archives. Research Guide on census returns (Domestic Records Information 99).

Locations and websites for the availability of census returns are listed in **Chapter 8**.

Electoral Lists

Gibson, J.S.W. and Rogers, C., *Electoral Registers since 1832 and Burgess Rolls* (Federation of Family History Societies, 1990)

Gibson, J.S.W. and Rogers, C., *Poll Books, 1696 to 1872* (Federation of Family History Societies, 1994).

Websites for the availability of electoral lists and poll books are listed in **Chapter 8**.

Trade Directories and Newspapers

Shaw, G. and Tipper, A., *British Directories: a Bibliography and Guide* (Leicester University Press, 1989)

Useful Websites

www.bl.uk/collections/newspapers.html

> (A vast collection of national and local newspapers.)

http://archive.timesonline.co.uk/tol/archive/

> (Another huge archive which can be word-searched from 1785 onwards.)

www.historicaldirectories.org
>(This site, maintained by the University of Leicester, contains a large and rapidly growing collection from directories between 1750 and 1920, including maps.)

CHAPTER 9: PROPERTY OWNERSHIP AND INHERITANCE

Wills

Collins, A., *Using Wills after 1858* (Federation of Family History Societies, 1998)

Gibson, J. and Churchill, E., *Probate Jurisdictions: Where to look in Wills* (Federation of Family History Societies, 2002).

Granum, K., *Using Wills* (Public Records Office, 2001)

McLaughlin, E., *Wills Before 1858* (Federation of Family History Societies, 1994)

Scott, M., *Prerogative Court of Canterbury: wills and other probate records* (Public Records Office, 1997)

Useful Websites

www.documentsonline.nationalarchives.gov.uk
>(Wills for the Prerogative Court of Canterbury can be viewed online and downloaded at a cost of £3 each.)

Other sources for indexes of wills are given in the text of **Chapter 9**.

Title Deeds

A Descriptive Catalogue of Ancient Deeds in the Public Records Office, 6 vols (HMSO, 1890-1906)

Alcock, N.W., *Old Title Deeds* (Phillimore, 2001)

Useful Website

www.catalogue.nationalarchives.gov.uk
>(Provides an index to enrolled deeds at the National Archives.)

www.landregistry.gov.uk/wps/portal/property_search

CHAPTER 10: MANORIAL AND ESTATE RECORDS

Ellis, M., *Using Manorial Records*, Readers Guide 6 (Public Records Office, 1994)

Harvey, P.D.A., *Manorial Records* (British Records Association, 1984)

Stuart, D., *Manorial Records: an Introduction to their Transcription and Translation* (Phillimore, 2004)

Useful Websites

www.medievalgeneology.org.uk
>(A useful catalogue of medieval source material on manorial documents available on-line.)

www.nationalarchives.gov.uk/mdr
>(Search for the Manorial Documents Register; also look for readers guides on aspects of manorial documents.)

CHAPTER 11: TAX RECORDS

Gibson, J., *Hearth Tax Returns and other Later Stuart Tax Lists and the Association Oath Rolls* (Federation of Family History Societies, 1996)

Gibson, J. *et al.*, *Land and Window Tax Assessments 1690-1950* (Federation of Family History Societies, 1997)

Jurkovski, M. *et al.*, *Lay Taxes in England and Wales* (Public Records Office, 1998)

Turner, M. and Mills, D. (eds), *Land and Property: The English Land Tax, 1692-1832* (Alan Sutton)

Useful websites
www.nationalarchives.gov.uk/e179/

(This website allows you to search for availability of hearth taxes for your parish.)

www.nationalarchives.gov.uk/e182/

(This deals with availability of window tax records.)

CHAPTER 12: MAPS, PLANS AND SURVEYS

General

Christian, P., 'Exploring Historical Maps Online', *Ancestors*, December 2004, pp.36-8

Foot, W., *Maps for Family History* (Public Records Office, 1994)

Harley, J.B., *Maps for the Local Historian: a Guide to British Sources* (National Council for Social Service, 1972)

Hindle, B.P., *Maps for Local History* (Batsford, 1998)

Public Records Office, *Maps and Plans in the British Isles 1410-1860* (1967)

Skelton, R.A. and Harvey, P.D.A., *Local Maps and Plans for Medieval England* (Clarendon Press, 1986)

Useful Websites
www.british-history.ac.uk

(A digital library giving access to 19th-century O.S. maps at large scales.)

www.nationalarchives.gov.uk

(See Research Guide on Maps in the National Archives.)

www.ordnancesurvey.co.uk

(For details of products and prices, including archive homepage, historical maps and early editions of O.S. mapping.)

www.visionofbritain.org.uk

(Post-code and place name searches are possible, giving access to 19th- and 20th-century maps).

Tithe Maps

Kain, R.J.P. and Prince, H.C., *The Tithe Surveys of England and Wales* (Cambridge University Press, 1985)

Kain, R.J.P. and Oliver, R.R., *The Tithe Maps and Apportionments of England and Wales* (Cambridge University Press, 1994)

Kain, R.J.P. and Oliver, R.R., *The Tithe Maps of England and Wales: A Cartographic Analysis and County-by-County Catalogue* (Cambridge University Press, 1995)

National Land Surveys

Barnwell, P.S., 'The National Farm Survey 1941-3', *Journal of the Historic Farm Buildings Group,* VII (1994)

Beech, G., 'The 20th-century Domesday Book*', Ancestors*, February 2005, p.36

Mitchell, R., The National Farm Survey, *Ancestors*, vol. 7, Apr/May 2002

Short, B., *The Geography of England in 1910: an Evaluation of Lloyd George's Domesday of Land Ownership* (Historical Geography Research Group, Institute of British Geographers, 1989)

Glossary

advowson – the right to appoint church livings (mainly posts for parish priests), often a hereditary right for the lord of the manor, exercised with the approval of the bishop, as a formality.

alienate – to transfer property away from the normal line of inheritance.

amercement – a financial penalty, e.g. for tenants failing to attend the manor court for no given reason.

arpent – a measure, imported from France, used in Domesday Book in relation to vineyards, an arpent being equivalent to 100 square perches.

bailiff – a person appointed by the lord of the manor to act as general estate manager and look after the day-to-day running of the manor.

barge boards – carved or fretted boards, fixed to the end of **purlins** at a gable.

bay – the portion of a framed building between the principal supporting timbers, often used as a unit to measure the length of a building, e.g. two-bay hall.

Bayleaf – the name of the **Wealden hall house** on display at the Weald and Downland Open Air Museum, relocated prior to the creation of Bough Beech Reservoir.

benefice – commonly used in the Church of England to describe a group of parishes under a single stipendiary minister.

box-framed – the form of construction in which roof **trusses** are carried on a frame composed of posts, **tie beams** and **wall plates.**

braces – curved or straight timber normally running between vertical and horizontal members of a frame.

campo – a field.

cartouche – the pictures and decorative designs in the titles and margins of maps.

cartularies – documentation on estates, assembled during Saxon times and at the time of Dissolution when monastic estates were transferred to private hands or the Crown.

charter – from the Latin *carta*, meaning paper, it is a document bestowing certain rights, such as land rights in the case of Anglo-Saxon charters.

clay-with-flints – a superficial deposit capping hills, especially on chalk rock, consisting of heavy brown clay with abundant flints, often left as woodland.

copyhold – 'unfree' land which was held according to the custom of the manor and transferred over time by the manorial court.

copyholder/customary holder – a manorial tenant who held land according to the custom of the manor, the tenant receiving a 'copy' of the court roll entry.

cottars or bordars – the humblest and poorest on the manor estate who held no land, but worked for the lord or prominent freeholders, often holding a cottage with a small garden.

court baron – laid down the rights and duties of the lord of the manor and his tenants, and recorded details of leases or tenancies.

court leet - a court dealing with petty offences under the manorial system, also responsible for maintenance of highways and ditches.

crop marks - variations in crop growth showing up on aerial photographs, often revealing the location of underground structures.

cross-passage - marks the position of the entrance to the house, and continues as a passage with a wall or partition towards the **hall**.

crown post - the upright timber standing on a **tie beam** in the roof space, which supports the roof.

dais bench - raised platform at the upper end, or **high end** of a hall.

dapifer - one who brings meat to the table, often the official title of the **steward** in the lord's household or royal court.

demesne - land reserved for the lord of the manor, for his own use.

dower - money or goods assigned to the bride as part of the marriage agreement. This occasionally included a dower house which became her residence if she was pre-deceased by her spouse.

down/downland - wide expanses of smooth, grassy hills on the chalk, such as the South Downs.

dry valley or coombe - a feature of chalk country, excavated by river action when the water table was higher, or when normally permeable chalk was frozen (Ice Age).

entry fine - a payment made upon an incoming customary tenant according to the custom of the manor.

escheator - an officer or royal official appointed to safeguard the rights of the Crown, when an **escheat** has taken place.

escheat - the reverting of property to the Crown when, for example, a tenant dies without heirs.

essoins - payments made by tenants to excuse their absence from a manorial court, the levy being fixed by the custom of the manor.

field system - the classification of collections of fields according to size, shape, orientation etc.

Flemish bond - an attractive and strong pattern of bricklaying with alternating stretchers and headers in the same course of bricks.

freehold land - land held from the lord of the manor on fixed terms.

gavelkind or **partible inheritance** - a system of land tenure associated chiefly with Kent, in which the estate descends not to the eldest son, but to all sons.

geophysical survey - the systematic collection of data, used for example in identifying archaeological features in advance of development.

hachures - the use of shading lines on maps to indicate slopes, eventually in time replaced by contours.

hall/open hall - the traditional name for the main living room of the house. An open hall was open from the floor to the roof ridge, with an open fire.

hall house - see **Wealden hall house**.

hayward - one who supervised the harvesting and making of hay on the lord's estates.

hereditament - a number allocated to a property for the purpose of land valuation, the boundary of the property being shown on an accompanying map.

hide - an Old English term, notionally the amount of land which could support a household, used as a unit of tax assessment in Domesday.

high end - the bay at one end of an **open hall** containing the parlour, as opposed to the low end, containing service rooms.

homage - the jury, made up of manorial tenants who served the court baron.

hundred ~ an administrative sub-division of a shire, with fiscal, judicial and military functions, notionally comprising 100 **hides**.

jetty or jettied gable ~ the cantilevered overhang of one storey above another, often seen in the **Wealden hall house**.

jowl post ~ the enlarged head at the top of a post to accommodate the housings for **wall plate** and **tie beam**.

knapped flint ~ flint shaped by striking the stone to produce flakes, or larger pieces of regularly shaped stone for building.

lath and daub ~ small timbers (laths), used as a partition, to which is applied crude forms of mortar (clay, straw, brickearth, cow dung).

lathe ~ a subdivision of a shire, exclusive to Kent.

lynchets ~ banks of earth running around contours that build up on the down slope of a field which has been ploughed for a long time, creating a series of terraces.

magnetometer ~ an instrument used to measure the strength of a magnetic field in detecting, for example, building lines below ground level.

manor ~ the traditional English estate unit, governed by fixed administrative procedures and dating back to Saxon times.

mark ~ not an actual coin, but a weight defining a unit of account, equivalent to 13s. 4d.

messuage/capital messuage ~ a term used in manorial documents for a house, the capital messuage being the main house (manor).

mullion ~ the vertical member between the lights in a window opening.

oriel window ~ a window which projects from the wall of a house and is supported by brackets, usually late- and post-16th-century.

palaeography ~ the study of writing in documents from the past.

plough land ~ an estimate of the arable capacity of an estate, in terms of the number of eight-ox **plough teams** needed to work it.

plough team ~ four pairs of oxen.

poll book ~ a list of freeholders, indicating the right of those eligible to vote.

precept ~ a notice issued to tenants by the **steward** of a manor, giving details of the court to be held.

Prerogative Court ~ the court which granted **probate** before 1858, one for the province of York, and the other for the province of Canterbury.

presentment ~ the point at which the **jury** of a manor court 'presented' the agenda, sometimes prepared and written out in advance.

primogeniture ~ the common law in which the first born son inherits the whole estate, to the exclusion of younger siblings.

probate ~ notification that a will has been **proved** in court.

probate inventory ~ inventories undertaken within a few days of death to protect the interests of any beneficiaries of the deceased.

prove a will ~ the formal approval of a will by the **Prerogative Court**, called a grant of probate.

purlin ~ longitudinal timbers running the length of the roof, between the **wall plate** and the ridge, giving support to common rafters (i.e. those which run from wall plate to ridge).

quit rent ~ the conversion of agricultural services to monetary payments.

rafters ~ timbers which run up the roof from wall plate to apex, supported by the wall plate and purlins.

reeve ~ one appointed to act as a foreman, with responsibility for overseeing the cultivation of land held by the lord of the manor.

regnal year ~ a method of dating, using the first day of a monarch's reign as the first day of the year, e.g. 1 James 1st, ran from 24 March 1603 to 23 March 1604.

relief ~ a cash payment to the lord of the manor made by the heir to, or purchaser of, **freehold land**, usually set at a value of one year's rent.

resistivity survey ~ attempts to measure the varying abilities of soils to conduct an electrical charge, particularly useful for locating building lines and sites of archaeological importance.

reversion ~ land that would revert to the original grantor at the end of the term was described as being held 'in reversion'.

river alluvium ~ sediments deposited by a river, typically composed of silt or clay, often providing good soils for agriculture.

river terrace ~ part of an old flood plain 'perched' on the side of a river valley, often fertile and used for dry settlement sites, being above flood levels.

service wing ~ the 'low end' of the manor house, adjacent to the **cross-passage** and containing the service rooms (the pantry and the buttery, for food and drink respectively).

shadow marks ~ shadows marking hollows and depressions, visible when the sun is low in the sky, thus revealing archaeological features on aerial photographs which are not apparent to the observer on the ground.

soil marks ~ variations in soil colour, observed from aerial photographs, which may reflect traces of archaeological features in ploughed fields.

stereoscopic viewer ~ a simple mechanism for viewing two vertical aerial photographs, each taken from a slightly different view point, to create a three-dimensional image.

steward ~ the chief administrator of the manor, who may have acted in this capacity for a group of his lord's manors.

sulung ~ a Kentish unit of assessment recorded in Domesday, usually regarded as being equivalent to two **hides**.

sworn men or **jurats** ~ responsible for the maintenance of drainage features, as on Romney Marsh.

tenant-in-chief ~ one who holds land direct from the Crown under a manorial system of landholding.

tie beam ~ the main transverse timber connecting the tops of the walls and **wall plates**.

tithe ~ a 'payment in kind', usually consisting of a tenth of annual produce of land, and paid to the parson of the parish.

tithe apportionment ~ a formal agreement that set a monetary value on **tithes** to be commuted for each parish. The total value was then allocated to liable individuals of the parish.

title deed ~ documentation used for past transfers of land and property, and which conveyed legal possession.

truss ~ a rigid transverse framework constructed across the roof at **bay** intervals to prevent the roof from spreading, and to carry longitudinal timbers or **purlins**.

undershot passage ~ cross-passage which lies immediately adjacent to the **hall** within the **service wing**, with the upper floor of the service wing extending over the passage.

view/view of frankpledge ~ a responsibility, devolved from the Crown to the lord of the manor, which involved overseeing good behaviour in households and the power to impose fines and try offences in the **court leet**.

vill ~ from the Latin *villa* (village), the lowest unit of local administration. Not necessarily a village in the modern sense, this represents an area of land rather than a settlement site.

villeins or bondmen ~ those who held land from the lord of the manor in return for rents, often obliged to assist with the cultivation of **demesne** lands.

wall plate ~ the timber on top of a wall frame or a masonry wall on which roof trusses and tie beams rest.

Wealden hall house ~ type of medieval house with an open **hall** and a two-storied **bay** at each end, and located generally, but not exclusively, in the Weald of Kent and Sussex.

yoke ~ in Kent, one quarter of a sulung. Oxen were yoked in pairs and a full **plough team** would have consisted of four pairs of oxen.

Index

Bold page numbers refer to tables or figures.